'Group of Palm Leaves' quilt motif surrounded by: 'Fleur-de-Lis' Edging, 'Valenciennes' Border, 'Wide Handsome' Border and 'Wide Open' Border.

ACKNOWLEDGMENT

I would like to thank Miss Ayliffe Hervey for her patient and careful work in knitting and checking the patterns in this book; Mrs Jacqueline Sandford for sending quilt patterns which have been in her family for many years, and Mrs Dixon for lending her family's 150 year old quilt to be photographed.

The metric and imperial measurements used in this book are not exact equivalents but are approximate equivalents. The metric and UK needle sizes are the nearest equivalents in the two systems. All the measurements given relate to a particular knitter's tension; please check your own tension with a test swatch.

C O N T E N T S

Page

ABBREVIATIONS

K	= knit
P	= purl
Sk	= slip one stitch knitwise
Sp	= slip one stitch purlwise
O	= one over (yarn over needle, yarn round needle)
c	= cast on
C	= cast off
M	= make one by lifting, twisting and knitting the yarn bar between two stitches, or any other solid increase
U	= turn, leaving stitches 'in holding' on the working needle To avoid a hole, before turning bring the yarn forward, slip the next stitch, take the yarn back, return the slipped stitch and now turn the work
K2tog	= knit two loops together as though knitting one stitch
SKtog	= slip one knitwise, knit one, pass slipped stitch over
K3tog	= knit three loops together as though knitting one stitch
SK2tog	= slip one knitwise, knit two together, pass slipped stitch over
SK3tog	= slip one knitwise, knit three together, pass slipped stitch over
P2tog	= purl two loops together as though purling one stitch
P3tog	= purl three loops together as though purling one stitch
*	= repeat instructions between asterisks until the last few stitches, or until the end of the row

If a number follows an abbreviation or a set of abbreviations in brackets, the action is repeated that number of times:

K6 = knit six stitches

(P2, K2tog)3 = purl two, knit two together, purl two, knit two together, purl two, knit two together

INTRODUCTION

Quilting – that is, sandwiching some sort of wadding between two
pieces of fabric and holding the three layers in place with functional
or decorative stitching – is a much-favoured, traditional craft. Patch-
work quilts, made by piecing together a number of small fabric shapes
and using the resultant large piece as one layer for a quilt, is another
very popular craft. Applique, the sewing of braid or fabric shapes
onto a piece of material used as the top layer of a quilt, is also a
form of the craft, and is often employed for all kinds of creative and
exciting needlework. But knitted quilts, though well known in the
Victorian salons in the form of counterpanes, sofa blankets, anti-
macassars and other knitted articles, have not recently had the
publicity they deserve.

Knitted quilts are made of all kinds of relatively small knitted shapes
and forms, and then assembled into a large piece, usually trimmed with
flounces, or frills. Perhaps the most fascinating aspect of these pieces
is that they are so often made in embossed or 'blister' knitting with a
variety of raised knitted forms decorating the shapes which are later
assembled into the completed quilt. Possibly the best-known use is for
bedspreads, or 'counterpanes', but the Victorians needed many types
of coverlet to keep them warm, and no doubt 'sofa blankets' were a
great help, but the knitted quilt was also useful for the horse-drawn
carriages, the baby carriages, or for shawls, cushion covers, and
even for curtains or free-standing draught excluders. Now that the
energy crisis is with us, we might do worse than revive the craft, for
the sake of warmth; but it is the decorative aspect with which this
book is primarily concerned.

GARDEN PLOT QUILTS

The original 'garden plot square' design was worked with a large leaf
shape set into one corner, and a row of smaller leaves spanning the
diagonal of the square, with ridge patterns completing the design. This
garden plot theme appeared in many variations, both in square and triangular shapes. 'Willow Leaf', 'Snowdrop' and 'Palm Leaves' were some
of the well-known names for beautiful designs. They could be assembled
into magnificent pieces of work, the result more like an art than a craft.
Most of these, and other types of lovely old quilt shape patterns, have not
been republished for many years. This book sets out to fill that void.

QUILT PIECE SHAPES

Perhaps the most common shape used for quilt pieces, then as now, is the 'square'; it's so common that many people refer to all quilt pieces as 'squares' without any regard to their actual shape.

Knitted quilt squares can be worked straight, by casting on a specific number of stitches and knitting the number of rows needed to equal the width of the piece. The work is cast off and the first square is finished. This type of square is worked in a similar way to a tension swatch, and can be made to any size and by any method of knitting. But this method of knitting a square does have a serious drawback: however carefully the tension is measured, the piece may eventually settle into a rectangular shape and throw the whole quilt design out of kilter.

A more stable shape is made by starting the square at a corner, with one or two stitches, increasing evenly at the beginning of each row, then decreasing in the same way to one or two stitches. The size of the square will be determined by the yarn used, the needle size or tension dial number chosen, the stitch pattern and the number of rows worked before the decrease rows are started. Many of the old patterns are worked in this way, often in an asymmetric design which is then reproduced three more times so that four pieces can be put together in two ways to make two motif squares. The 'Corinthian' design has been used to make both the front and back cover illustrations. Provided the pieces are properly assembled, the patterns within the large motif square make new shapes, so that it's not just the original small design which is important, it's also the way the pieces are assembled. A complete 'Corinthian' quilt can be built up in either way and, though both motifs appear in a single colour quilt, the way the patterns are seen depends on which way the central pieces are assembled. There's also scope for using several colours and, provided the tensions are very carefully checked, one can mix patterned, textured and plain pieces of the same size. The colours and textures can be varied by making individual shapes in different colours, or by knitting one piece so that one colour or texture is used for one half of the square, say, and another to finish it.

Triangle shapes are almost as popular as squares, and for the very good reason that a square, halved by cutting it from corner to corner, will form two equal triangles. There's something to be said for starting with one or two stitches and making two triangles, then joining them, with grafting, latch-up or sewing, for those patterns which are suited to this method – it avoids the difference between increasing and decreasing at or inside the slanting side selvedges.

Triangle shapes can be assembled into quilts in a number of ways, and they need not always be right-angled triangles. Equilateral triangles (all sides equal) make interesting variations possible, and two examples of a simple triangle pattern assembled into two different shapes are shown in the 'Ridged Hexagon' and 'Open Shell' patterns.

The relatively small size of the pattern shapes makes for comfortable hand knitting; there's no need for heavy and cumbersome work, and only one pattern need be learned even for an impressive-looking quilt. The shapes can also be combined with rapidly worked machine knitted shapes or strips, so that the whole project need not take too long. However, the way the pieces are assembled and tensioned is what makes one quilt beautiful or mars another. The old patterns do not give instructions on how to join the pieces or how to prepare them before joining them. The following suggestions are illustrated in some of the patterns.

'LOOP' SELVEDGES

An essential part of any method of assembling and tensioning knitted pieces is the selvedges of the pieces to be joined. One of the advantages of starting the knitting with one or two stitches and increasing at the beginning of every row is that it's so easy to make a simple picot edge. For hand work, the yarn is wrapped round the needle before the first stitch in the row is knitted, and for machine work a new needle is brought out into the working position. The edge loop formed in this way can be enlarged in both hand and machine knitting. The yarn can be wrapped round the needle more than once, or more than one needle can be brought forward to knit a larger increase stitch, the extra needles being pushed back again once the row has been knitted. A neat, adjustable size loop is produced by all methods. The bias squares, which are made by decreasing after the central row, can still have side loops, though a double decrease will have to be worked for each row, and any method of doing this can be used. The picots can be made the same size as those used for the increase rows, but the actual decreases themselves will show as a ridge, so that there will be a difference between the two sections.

Picots can also be made for straight pieces of knitting by combining a picot with a single decrease at the beginning of each row. Another possibility is to drop the first and last stitches at the end of a knitted strip, to allow these stitches to unravel, and so form side loops. Pieces can be started and ended with open loops, so that all selvedges are 'loop' selvedges.

SHAPING AND TENSIONING

An even tension is important for all knitting, but vital when making large numbers of small pieces to be assembled later. This isn't a problem in machine knitting, of course. However, even the neatest hand knitter will not end up with pieces which are ready, as such, for assembling into a quilt, and machine knitted shapes, too, will need 'dressing'. The illustration of the 'Mulberry-Leaf' square shows the startling difference before and after shaping the piece.

Assuming the knitting tension is even, the next step is to make a guide to the shape the piece is to be. In the first place, one needs a definite shape which can be adjusted to produce the correct size. Let's use a knitted square as an example. Squares are not difficult to draw, but I think it's a mistake to draw a square and then to knit to this size. If the pattern is designed to end up as a square shape, the actual size of the square will depend on the yarn and needle, or tension setting, used as well as on the stitch pattern and the individual knitter – all highly variable components.

A metre or yard stick is invaluable for drawing long lines on large paper, card or plastic surfaces. Draw two lines to cross at right angles, in the middle of the surface. Mark off equal lengths of, say, 5 cm, outwards from the central cross. If necessary, set this guide on a suitably protected carpeted floor, ready for having the knitted square shape pinned onto it.

Though it's relatively easy to set any knitted shape onto a pre-drawn, accurate outline, it isn't always easy to produce a completely straight edge. However, if each selvedge is threaded onto an adequately long, reasonably fine, knitting needle, or the needle left in the last knitted row, the shape can readily be tensioned. This is where the 'loop' edges are so very helpful. Suitably moisten or starch the knitted piece, put a pin through the centre of the design, and place this at the intersection of the two drawn lines. Place and pin the corners of the piece on the four drawn spokes, at equal distances from the centre. Move the corners out, equally, as much as possible, and set pins to hold the knitting needles in the correct positions. Allow the square to dry, moving the corners out further after an interval of one or two hours if they seem to need it. When the square is completely taut and dry, take it off the needles – first and last row open loops will not run if they are starched. Now measure it. That is your proper tension. All other squares should be 'dressed' to this size.

Tension all your shapes on this basis. It's easiest to start shaping from the centre out, and to pin the corners onto suitable guidelines. Provided you pin at equal distances from the centre, you will get a regular shape.

This procedure sees to the shape of the quilt piece, but it does nothing for the 'blisters' which are such an attractive feature of many of the patterns. If left to themselves, the 'blisters' will not show to full advantage, as you can see from the illustration overleaf. There is a way round this. Find a suitable button, bead or other mould, starch the quilt piece, and place your moulds under the 'blisters'. Now smooth the fabric over the mould and pin in position. All the 'blister' quilt patterns illustrated in this book were dressed in this way.

ASSEMBLING

Many knitters intensely dislike 'making up', that is the assembly, usually by sewing, of knitted pieces into the finished article. The assembling of the quilt pieces is as much part of the work as the knitting; it's not only important, it will distinguish one knitter's work from another's and will considerably enhance the effect of the beautiful patterns if carried out in an appropriate and meticulous way.

Assembling quilt shapes made with 'looped' selvedges is relatively simple, and doesn't necessarily involve sewing. One of the quickest methods is to use a crochet hook or latchet tool, and large selvedge loops. Insert the hook in the first loop on one side, pull the first loop from the other side through it, then continue by pulling through the next loop from the first side and so on, all the way along the two selvedges to be connected. As each loop is used to make a new stitch, it needs to be relatively large to make a join in keeping with the rest of the work.

Small picot or other loops can be joined by grafting; this is a very success-ful method of joining the edges, and, once one gets used to it, very quick. It's hard to tell where one piece finishes and another ends, as shown in the 'Lily' pattern.

Crochet can also be used to join loop edges, and many forms of embroidery or just flat or oversew stitch are also suitable. The loops make it easy to join the correct stitches, and all the work will be reversible. Given the right pattern, the whole quilt can be made reversible. As all the knitted shapes will have been dressed before they are joined, one can set the pieces in position, ready for assembly, on a bed or a covered floor. The

quilt joins can then be 'dressed' by moistening them with water or a
starching medium, so that the whole quilt is treated in the same way.
The completed quilt can be left to dry to the correct shape on the
floor or the bed.

FRILLS AND FLOUNCES

However beautifully the individual pieces may have been knitted and
assembled, the completed quilt will lack 'finish' if it has no border.
Quilts assembled and finished so that the corners are right-angled
look well with mitred finishing flounces. One will often have to work
out the mitre oneself, though the 'Chain Pattern Fringe' has instructions for a mitred corner in full. A less complicated method is to
gather one of the shallower edging patterns at the corner, as shown
for the 'Armenian' lace used on the 'Open Ribbed' pattern and illustrated
on page 57, or to use one of the flounces with an inherent ruffle, such
as the 'Scallop' edging. If deep, straight flounces are preferred, one
might consider knitting a special square to fit between straight pieces of
edging. An example has been worked out for the Corinthian pattern, and
this is illustrated on page 55. Yet another solution is to finish the corners
by leaving out half of a pattern square, as illustrated with the 'Snowdrop'
pattern and the 'Raised Leaf' border on page 2.

The raised 'Snowdrop' pattern is shown
with moulds inserted under the 'blisters'
in the top part, and without any moulds
in the bottom part.

YARNS

Most of the quilt patterns in this book date from the 'white knitting' period of the nineteenth century. The material used for making the quilts was primarily white cotton yarn of various thicknesses. The type of cotton yarn readily available now varies between a 20s crochet cotton and the chunky 'handicraft' cotton. All these make excellent and hardwearing quilts, but, if you prefer to knit with one of the many new cottons now available from specialist suppliers you can substitute these. My YARNS FOR THE KNITTER (Thorn, 1980) gives details of yarn sizing systems and shows you how to compare the cotton count with the worsted or metric count used for most wool and synthetic knitting yarns. This book also explains how to relate these counts to the usual ply numbers.

Perhaps the most important thing about knitting quilts is to choose a fairly small needle size or tension dial number relative to the yarn. The combinations used for the illustrated patterns are mentioned in the text. These should produce a sufficiently firm material which will display the patterns effectively as well as produce the right tension to make the correct shape. It's always best to work a test swatch to establish that your individual tension will give satisfactory results.

It is, of course, possible to use wool to make the quilts. If you wish to use wool for the patterned shapes I think the modern 'machine washable' wools will be better than the more elastic and resilient 'natural' wools; the smoother and less elastic the yarn, the better you will be able to see the patterns.

Silk, rayon and synthetic yarns can all be used, and the 'Snowdrop' pattern, illustrated on page 2, was knitted in two colours of a synthetic 4-ply yarn. Mixtures of various fibres and textures can produce exciting designs even for plain knitted quilt shapes. The square illustrated on the inside front cover was knitted in garter stitch in a bulky chenille yarn. 'Willow Leaf' pattern was knitted in a 'thermal' yarn. It's very important to wash the shapes and then to tension them in order to establish precisely how the different fibres will combine in one quilt once the pieces are joined together. This precaution will avoid the making of disappointing 'mixed' knitted quilts.

MACHINE KNITTING

This book is primarily concerned with hand knitted quilt pattern motifs. However, the basic shapes used for the traditional knitted quilt pieces are readily made on the machine. The 'blister' stitch patterns are not so readily made by machine, and are outside the scope of this book, but machine stitch patterns can be used to very good effect. The machine knitted pieces can be mixed with hand knitted pieces or used to make machine knitted quilts. Patterns for 8 machine knitted edgings are given in my KNITTED LACE EDGINGS (Thorn, 1981), together with patterns for 19 hand knitted edgings.

MACHINE KNITTED TRIANGLE

Cast on one stitch.

For automatic pattern knitting, insert a design card into the machine and lock it on the appropriate row. Set the card into the machine memory, then release the card.

For all machine knitting, bring one needle forward from the non-working position, thus increasing by one stitch, and knit across the two stitches. Increase in this way at the beginning of every row, every alternate row, or any other suitable regular row sequence, until you have the number of stitches you require. Take the work off onto a knitting needle, or cast off, loosely, by any method.

MACHINE KNITTED DIAMOND

Knit as for the triangle but, instead of casting off or taking the work off the machine, continue knitting by decreasing at the start of every row, or any other row sequence, until only one stitch remains. Fasten off.

TENSION

The type of triangle or diamond made by these methods will depend on the tension at which the pieces are worked. The distances between opposite corners must be equal to make a square, rather than a diamond, shape. So, if one is making a square by increasing at the beginning of every row from 1 to 71 stitches, then decreasing to 1 stitch, say, 140 rows will be worked altogether. The tension needed will therefore mean that 71 stitches and 140 rows will both produce the same measurement over the knitted fabric.

PICOT SELVEDGES

The simple machine increase will give a small picot edge at the sides. For an equivalent picot at the decrease sides, take a double headed transfer tool, lift two stitches at the beginning of each decrease row over the next two stitches, leave one empty needle next to the needles in the working position, and return the other empty needle to the non-working position.

QUANTITIES AND SIZES

Obviously, the amount of yarn needed for a particular quilt will depend on the thickness of the yarn chosen, the size of the needles or tension dial number used, the stitch pattern worked and the size of the quilt. This last is conveniently based on using the main motif as a unit. An example has been worked out for the 'Corinthian' pattern, worked in Twilley's Handicraft No 1:

Each pattern motif, made up of 4 small squares, weighs 325 gm (12 0z) and measures 64 cm (25") square.

A quilt measuring roughly 190 cm (75") by 260 cm (100"), without an edging, would be made up of 3 x 4 motifs, that is 12 motif squares. These will weigh 12 x 325 gm (12 0z) or 3,900 gm (144 0z).

To surround the above quilt with the 'Ivy' pattern would require 900 cm (360") of this pattern. 30 cm (12") lengths weigh 30 gm (1 0z), so that 900 cm (360") would weigh 900 gm (30 0z).

That still leaves the corners unaccounted for; assume they will be filled by the 4 small squares based on the 'Corinthian' pattern, and that these weigh 30 gm (1 0z) each.

The total yarn required will be 4,920 gm (178 0z). That is, you will need roughly 5 kilos or 11 lb of the No 1 Handicraft cotton to make a complete quilt of this size.

These are, of course, approximate amounts. You will need to make your own square and flounce length to determine your own quantities.

I have given approximate amounts of the particular yarn used to make the patterns illustrated in this book. I have used readily obtainable materials, but you can substitute other yarn provided you check the tension carefully so that you produce the correct shape needed for the quilt design.

Work on a pair of needles   Twilley's Lyscordet No 5, 2.75 mm (12) needles:
Cast on 1 stitch   26 cm (10½") square took 30 gm (1 Oz) yarn

Let X = K2, 0, K2tog; M = knit into the back and front of the stitch

Row 1: 0, M   Row 2: 0, K3
Row 3: 0, K4   Row 4: 0, K5
Row 5: 0, K6   Row 6: 0, K7
Row 7: 0, K8   Row 8: 0, K9
Row 9: 0, K10   Row 10: 0, K11
Row 11: 0, K12   Row 12: 0, K13
Row 13: 0, K14   Row 14: 0, K15
Row 15: 0, K16   Row 16: 0, K17
Row 17: 0, K18   Row 18: 0, K19

Row 19: 0, K20	Row 20: 0, K21
Row 21: 0, K22	Row 22: 0, K23
Row 23: 0, K1, P23	Row 24: 0, X6, K1
Row 25: 0, K1, P25	Row 26: 0, K27
Row 27: 0, K1, P27	Row 28: 0, X7, K1
Row 29: 0, K1, P29	Row 30: 0, K31
Row 31: 0, K1, P31	Row 32: 0, X8, K1
Row 33: 0, K1, P33	Row 34: 0, K35
Row 35: 0, K36	Row 36: 0, K37
Row 37: 0, K38	Row 38: 0, K39
Row 39: 0, K40	Row 40: 0, K41
Row 41: 0, K42	Row 42: 0, K2tog, K41
Row 43: 0, K2tog, K41	Row 44: 0, K3tog, K40
Row 45: 0, K3tog, K39	Row 46: 0, K3tog, K38
Row 47: 0, K3tog, K37	Row 48: 0, K3tog, K36
Row 49: 0, K3tog, K35	Row 50: 0, K3tog, K34
Row 51: 0, K3tog, P33	Row 52: 0, K3tog, K1, 0, K2tog, X7, K1
Row 53: 0, K3tog, P31	Row 54: 0, K3tog, K30
Row 55: 0, K3tog, P29	Row 56: 0, K3tog, K1, 0, K2tog, X6, K1
Row 57: 0, K3tog, P27	Row 58: 0, K3tog, K26
Row 59: 0, K3tog, P25	Row 60: 0, K3tog, K1, 0, K2tog, X5, K1
Row 61: 0, K3tog, P23	Row 62: 0, K3tog, K22
Row 63: 0, K3tog, K21	Row 64: 0, K3tog, K20
Row 65: 0, K3tog, K19	Row 66: 0, K3tog, K18
Row 67: 0, K3tog, K17	Row 68: 0, K3tog, K16
Row 69: 0, K3tog, K15	Row 70: 0, K3tog, K14
Row 71: 0, K3tog, K13	Row 72: 0, K3tog, K12
Row 73: 0, K3tog, K11	Row 74: 0, K3tog, K10
Row 75: 0, K3tog, K9	Row 76: 0, K3tog, K8
Row 77: 0, K3tog, K7	Row 78: 0, K3tog, K6
Row 79: 0, K3tog, K5	Row 80: 0, K3tog, K4
Row 81: 0, K3tog, K3	Row 82: 0, K3tog, K2
Row 83: 0, K3tog, K1	Row 84: 0, K3tog; fasten off

PATTERN REPEAT:
Knit 3 more squares to form a large square

The average knitting time for each square was 1 hour. This is an easy, but effective pattern. Knitting rows 22 – 33 and rows 50 – 61 inclusive in a different colour increases the pattern possibilities.

APPLE-LEAF PATTERN

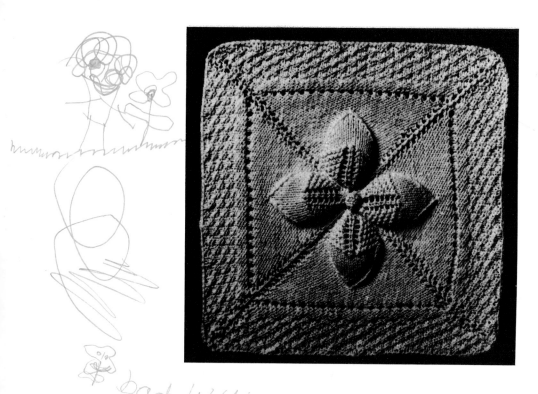

Work on a pair of needles
Cast on 3 stitches

Start EACH row with either (0, K1) or (02, K1), depending on the size of picot you wish to achieve.

Row 1: 0, K1, 0, K1
Row 3: P2, 0, K1, 0, P3
Row 5: P4, 0, K1, 0, P5
Row 7: P6, 0, K1, 0, P7
Row 9: P8, 0, K1, 0, P9
Row 11: P10, 0, K1, 0, P11
Row 13: P12, 0, K1, 0, P13
Row 15: P14, 0, K1, 0, P15

Row 2: P3, K2
Row 4: K1, P5, K3
Row 6: K2, P7, K4
Row 8: K3, P9, K5
Row 10: K4, P11, K6
Row 12: K5, P13, K7
Row 14: K6, P15, K8
Row 16: K7, P17, K9

16

Sl. k1. psso = Sk tog

Row 17:	P8, SKtog, K13, K2tog, P9	Row 18:	K8, P15, K10
Row 19:	P9, SKtog, K11, K2tog, P10	Row 20:	K9, P13, K11
Row 21:	P10, SKtog, K9, K2tog, P11	Row 22:	K10, P11, K12
Row 23:	P11, SKtog, K7, K2tog, P12	Row 24:	K11, P9, K13
Row 25:	P12, SKtog, K5, K2tog, P13	Row 26:	K12, P7, K14
Row 27:	P13, SKtog, K3, K2tog, P14	Row 28:	K13, P5, K15
Row 29:	P14, SKtog, K1, K2tog, P15	Row 30:	K14, P3, K16
Row 31:	P15, SK2tog, P16	Row 32:	K15, P1, K17
Row 33:	P34	Row 34:	K35
Row 35:	P36	Row 36:	K37
Row 37:	P38	Row 38:	P39
Row 39:	(0, K2tog) 20	Row 40:	P41
Row 41:	P41, M1, P1	Row 42:	K44
Row 43:	P45	Row 44:	K46
Row 45:	K1, P2, (K2, P2)11	Row 46:	K1, P2, (K2, P2)11, K1
Row 47:	(P2, K2)12, P1	Row 48:	P2, (K2, P2)12
Row 49:	P1, K2, (P2, K2)12	Row 50:	P1, K2, (P2, K2)12, P1
Row 51:	(K2, P2)13, K1	Row 52:	(K2, P2) 13, K2
Row 53:	K1, P2, (K2, P2)13	Row 54:	K1, P2, (K2, P2)13, K1
Row 55:	(P2, K2)14, P1	Row 56:	P2, (K2, P2) 14
Row 57:	P1, K2, (P2, K2)14	Row 58:	P1, K2, (P2, K2)14, P1

Cast off, or hold stitches on a needle till ready to graft to another piece.

PATTERN REPEAT:
Knit 3 more triangles to form a square.

Twilley's Stalite No 3, 2.75 (12) needles: 26 cm (10½") square took 60 gm (2 Oz) yarn

Each triangle took an average of 1 hour and 20 minutes to knit. The four large apple leaves will need a mould inserted from underneath to bring out the shape. A small bobble has been added in the centre; this can be used for decorative purposes only or, if a backed quilt is to be made, the bobble can be sewn through all layers to hold them together.

The four triangles in the illustration have been assembled by pulling one picot through another with the tip of a threaded tapestry needle, pulling the thread through after each crossing. This method is often used by the Shetland Island knitters to connect sections of their shawls, as it gives an eyelet effect.

BAY-LEAF PATTERN

Work on a pair of needles
Cast on 3 stitches

Twilley's Stalite No 3, 2.75 mm (12) needles:
28 cm (11") square took 75 gm (2½ Oz) yarn

Row 1: K1, M, K1, M, K1

Row 2: Sp, K4

Row 3: Sp, K1, M, K1, M, K2

Row 4: Sp, K6

Row 5: Sp, K2, O, K1, O, K3

Row 6: Sp, K2, P3, K3

Row 7: Sp, K2, O, K3, O, K3

Row 8: Sp, K2, P5, K3

Row 9: Sp, K2, O, K5, O, K3

Row 10: Sp, K2, P7, K3

Row 11: Sp, K2, O, P7, O, K3

Row 12: Sp, K14

Row 13: Sp, K2, O, P9, O, K3

Row 14: Sp, K16

Row 15: Sp, K2, O, K11, O, K3

Row 16: Sp, K2, P13, K3

Row 17: Sp, K2, O, K13, O, K3

Row 18: Sp, K2, P15, K3

Row 19: Sp, K2, O, P15, O, K3

Row 20: Sp, K22

Row 21: Sp, K2, O, P17, O, K3

Row 22: Sp, K24

Row 23: Sp, K2, 0, K19, 0, K3   Row 24: Sp, K2, P21, K3
Row 25: Sp, K2, 0, K21, 0, K3   Row 26: Sp, K2, P23, K3
Row 27: Sp, K2, 0, P23, 0, K3   Row 28: Sp, K30
Row 29: Sp, K2, 0, P25, 0, K3   Row 30: Sp, K32
Row 31: Sp, K2, 0, K27, 0, K3   Row 32: Sp, K2, P29, K3
Row 33: Sp, K2, 0, K29, 0, K3   Row 34: Sp, K2, P31, K3
Row 35: Sp, K2, 0, P31, 0, K3   Row 36: Sp, K38
Row 37: Sp, K2, 0, P33, 0, K3   Row 38: Sp, K40
Row 39: Sp, K2, 0, K35, 0, K3   Row 40: Sp, K2, P37, K3
Row 41: Sp, K2, 0, K37, 0, K3   Row 42: Sp, K2, P39, K3
Row 43: Sp, K2, 0, P39, 0, K3   Row 44: Sp, K46
Row 45: Sp, K2, 0, P41, 0, K3   Row 46: Sp, K48
Row 47: Sp, K2, 0, K43, 0, K3   Row 48: Sp, K2, P45, K3
Row 49: Sp, K2, 0, K45, 0, K3   Row 50: Sp, K2, P47, K3
Row 51: Sp, K2, 0, P2, (0, K1, 0, P6)6, 0, K1, 0, P2, 0, K3
Row 52: Sp, K5, (P3, K6)7
Row 53: Sp, K2, 0, P3, (0, K3, 0, P6)6, 0, K3, 0, P3, 0, K3
Row 54: Sp, K6, (P5, K6)7, K1
Row 55: Sp, K2, 0, P4, (0, K5, 0, P6)6, 0, K5, 0, P4, 0, K3
Row 56: Sp, K7, (P7, K6)7, K2
Row 57: Sp, K2, 0, P5, (0, K7, 0, P6)6, 0, K7, 0, P5, 0, K3
Row 58: Sp, K8, (P9, K6)7, K3
Row 59: Sp, K2, 0, P6, (K3, SK2tog, K3, P6)7, 0, K3
Row 60: Sp, K9, (P7, K6)7, K4
Row 61: Sp, K2, 0, P7, (K2, SK2tog, K2, P6)7, P1, 0, K3
Row 62: Sp, K10, (P5, K6)7, K5
Row 63: Sp, K2, 0, P8, (K1, SK2tog, K1, P6)7, P2, 0, K3
Row 64: Sp, K11, (P3, K6)7, K6
Row 65: Sp, K2, 0, P9, (SK2tog, P6)7, P3, 0, K3
Row 66: Sp, K12, (P1, K6)7, K7
Row 67: Sp, K2, (0, K2tog)30, 0, K3tog, 0, K3
Row 68: Sp, K68

Cast off or hold stitches on needle for grafting or tensioning.

PATTERN REPEAT:
Knit 3 more triangles to form a square

Each triangle took an average knitting time of 1 hour and 40 minutes. It's important to bring out the shapes of the bay leaves when tensioning the piece.

CORINTHIAN PATTERN

This richly patterned square took an average of $4\frac{1}{2}$ hours to knit.
Two different designs can be seen when the 'large' squares are joined,
depending on which way they are assembled. The front and back covers
show the two designs. An example of a small 'knob' square is given at
the end of the pattern; this can be used to 'turn the corner' when straight
edgings are used to border the completed quilt. The size of the 'knob'
square can be adjusted to fit the depth of the edging used.

Knit on a pair of needles Twilley's Handicraft No 1, 3.5 mm (10) needles:
Cast on 2 stitches 64 cm (25") large square took 325 gm (12 Oz) yarn

MK = make a knob as follows:
    (0, K1)3 ALL in the first stitch; U:P6; U:Sp, K5;
    U:Sk, P5; U:Sp, K5; U:(P2tog)3; U:SK2tog
    Keep the knob in front of the work and continue the row

Row 1: K2	Row 2: 0, K2
Row 3: 0, K2tog, M, K1	Row 4: 0, K2tog, K2
Row 5: 0, K2tog, 0, K2	Row 6: 0, K2tog, K3
Row 7: 0, K2tog, (0, K1)2, K1	Row 8: 0, K2tog, K5
Row 9: 0, K2tog, 0, K3, 0, K2	Row 10: 0, K2tog, K7
Row 11: 0, K2tog, 0, K5, 0, K2	Row 12: 0, K2tog, K9
Row 13: 0, K2tog, 0, K7, 0, K2	Row 14: 0, K2tog, K11
Row 15: 0, K2tog, 0, K9, 0, K2	Row 16: 0, K2tog, K13

Start raised knobs:

Row 17: 0, K2tog, 0, K5, MK, K5, 0, K2	Row 18: 0, K2tog, K15
Row 19: 0, K2tog, 0, K13, 0, K2	Row 20: 0, K2tog, K17
Row 21: 0, K2tog, 0, K5, MK, K3, MK, K5, 0, K2	Row 22: 0, K2tog, K19
Row 23: 0, K2tog, 0, K17, 0, K2	Row 24: 0, K2tog, K21
Row 25: 0, K2tog, 0, K5, (MK,K3)3, K2, 0, K2	Row 26: 0, K2tog, K23
Row 27: 0, K2tog, 0, K21, 0, K2	Row 28: 0, K2tog, K25
Row 29: 0, K2tog, 0, K9, MK, K3, MK, K9, 0, K2	Row 30: 0, K2tog, K27
Row 31: 0, K2tog, 0, K25, 0, K2	Row 32: 0, K2tog, K29
Row 33: 0, K2tog, 0, K13, MK, K13, 0, K2	Row 34: 0, K2tog, K31
Row 35: 0, K2tog, 0, K29, 0, K2	Row 36: 0, K2tog, K33
Row 37: 0, K2tog, 0, K31, 0, K2	Row 38: 0, K2tog, P33, K2
Row 39: 0, K2tog, 0, K33, 0, K2	Row 40: 0, K2tog, K37
Row 41: 0, K2tog, 0, P35, 0, K2	Row 42: 0, K2tog, K39
Row 43: 0, K2tog, 0, K37, 0, K2	Row 44: 0, K2tog, P39, K2
Row 45: 0, K2tog, 0, K39, 0, K2	Row 46: 0, K2tog, P41, K2

Start wheat-ears:

Row 47: 0, K2tog, 0, P2, (0, K1, 0, P5)6, 0, K1, 0, P2, 0, K2
Row 48: 0, K2tog, K3, (P3, K5)7
Row 49: 0, K2tog, 0, P3, (0, K3, 0, P5)6, 0, K3, 0, P3, 0, K2
Row 50: 0, K2tog, K4, (P5, K5)7, K1
Row 51: 0, K2tog, 0, P4, (0, K1, SK2tog, K1, 0, P5)6, 0, K1, SK2tog, K1, 0, P4, 0, K2
Row 52: 0, K2tog, K5, (P5, K5)7, K2
Row 53: 0, K2tog, 0, P5, (0, K1, SK2tog, K1, 0, P5)7, 0, K2
Row 54: 0, K2tog, K6, (P5, K5)7, K3
Row 55: 0, K2tog, 0, P6, (0, K1, SK2tog, K1, 0, P5)7, P1, 0, K2
Row 56: 0, K2tog, K7, (P5, K5)7, K4
Row 57: 0, K2tog, 0, P7, (0, K1, SK2tog, K1, 0, P5)7, P2, 0, K2
Row 58: 0, K2tog, K8, (P5, K5)7, K5
Row 59: 0, K2tog, 0, P8, (K1, SK2tog, K1, P5)7, P3, 0, K2
Row 60: 0, K2tog, K9, (P3, K5)7, K6
Row 61: 0, K2tog, 0, P9, (SK2tog, P5)7, P4, 0, K2
Row 62: 0, K2tog, P57, K2

Start ridge pattern and line of holes:

Row 63: 0, K2tog, 0, K57, 0, K2	Row 64: 0, K2tog, P59, K2
Row 65: 0, K2tog, 0, K59, 0, K2	Row 66: 0, K2tog, K63
Row 67: 0, K2tog, 0, P61, 0, K2	Row 68: 0, K2tog, K65
Row 69: 0, K2tog, 0, K63, 0, K2	Row 70: 0, K2tog, P65, K2
Row 71: 0, K2tog, 0, K2, (0, K2tog)31, K1, 0, K2	Row 72: 0, K2tog, K67, K2
Row 73: 0, K2tog, 0, K67, 0, K2	Row 74: 0, K2tog, K71
Row 75: 0, K2tog, 0, P69, 0, K2	Row 76: 0, K2tog, K73
Row 77: 0, K2tog, 0, K71, 0, K2	Row 78: 0, K2tog, P73, K2
Row 79: 0, K2tog, 0, K73, 0, K2	Row 80: 0, K2tog, P75, K2

Line of raised knobs, centre of square:

Row 81:   0, K2tog, 0, K2tog, MK, (K4, MK)14, K2tog, 0, K2

Row 82:   0, K2tog, P75, K2
Row 83:   0, SK2tog, 0, K2tog, K69, SKtog, 0, K2tog, K1
Row 84:   0, K2tog, P73, K2
Row 85:   0, SK2tog, 0, K2tog, K67, SKtog, 0, K2tog, K1
Row 86:   0, K2tog, K73
Row 87:   0, SK2tog, 0, P2tog, P65, P2tog, 0, K2tog, K1
Row 88:   0, K2tog, K71
Row 89:   0, SK2tog, 0, K2tog, K63, SKtog, 0, K2tog, K1
Row 90:   0, K2tog, P67, K2
Row 91:   0, SK2tog, (0, K2tog)31, 0, SK2tog, 0, K2tog, K1
Row 92:   0, K2tog, P65, K2
Row 93:   0, SK2tog, 0, K2tog, K59, SKtog, 0, K2tog, K1
Row 94:   0, K2tog, K65
Row 95:   0, SK2tog, 0, P2tog, P57, P2tog, 0, K2tog, K1
Row 96:   0, K2tog, K63
Row 97:   0, SK2tog, 0, K2tog, K55, SKtog, 0, K2tog, K1
Row 98:   0, K2tog, P59, K2
Row 99:   0, SK2tog, 0, K2tog, K53, SKtog, 0, K2tog, K1

Start open diamond pattern:

Row 100:   0, K2tog, P57, K2
Row 101:   0, SK2tog, 0, K2tog, K2, K2tog, (0, K1, 0, SKtog, K1, K2tog)7, 0, K1, 0, SKtog, K2, SKtog, 0, K2tog, K1
Row 102:   0, K2tog, P55, K2
Row 103:   0, SK2tog, 0, (K2tog)2, (0, K3, 0, SK2tog)7, 0, K3, 0, (SKtog)2, 0, K2tog, K1
Row 104:   0, K2tog, P53, K2
Row 105:   0, SK2tog, 0, K2tog, (0, SKtog, K1, K2tog, 0, K1)7, 0, SKtog, K1, K2tog, 0, SKtog, 0, K2tog, K1
Row 106:   0, K2tog, P51, K2
Row 107:   0, SK2tog, 0, K2tog, (0, SK2tog, 0, K3)7, 0, SK2tog, 0, SKtog, 0, K2tog, K1
Row 108:   0, K2tog, P49, K2
Row 109:   0, SK2tog, 0, K2tog, K1, (0, SKtog, K1, K2tog, 0, K1)7, SKtog, 0, K2tog, K1
Row 110:   0, K2tog, P47, K2
Row 111:   0, SK2tog, 0, K2tog, K1, (0, SK2tog, 0, K3)6, 0, SK2tog, 0, K1, SKtog, 0, K2tog, K1
Row 112:   0, K2tog, P45, K2
Row 113:   0, SK2tog, 0, K2tog, K2, (0, SKtog, K1, K2tog, 0, K1)6, K1, SKtog, 0, K2tog, K1
Row 114:   0, K2tog, P43, K2
Row 115:   0, SK2tog, 0, K2tog, K2, (0, SK2tog, 0, K3)5, 0, SK2tog, 0, K2, SKtog, 0, K2tog, K1
Row 116:   0, K2tog, P41, K2
Row 117:   0, SK2tog, 0, K2tog, K35, SKtog, 0, K2tog, K1
Row 118:   0, K2tog, P39, K2
Row 119:   0, SK2tog, 0, K2tog, K33, SKtog, 0, K2tog, K1
Row 120:   0, K2tog, K39
Row 121:   0, SK2tog, 0, P2tog, P31, P2tog, 0, K2tog, K1
Row 122:   0, K2tog, K37
Row 123:   0, SK2tog, 0, K2tog, K29, SKtog, 0, K2tog, K1
Row 124:   0, K2tog, P33, K2
Row 125:   0, SK2tog, 0, K2tog, K27, SKtog, 0, K2tog, K1
Row 126:   0, K2tog, K33
Row 127:   0, SK2tog, 0, K2tog, K25, SKtog, 0, K2tog, K1
Row 128:   0, K2tog, K31

Start raised knobs:

Row 129: 0, SK2tog, 0, K2tog, K11, MK, K11, SKtog, 0, K2tog, K1
Row 130: 0, K2tog, K29
Row 131: 0, SK2tog, 0, K2tog, K21, SKtog, 0, K2tog, K1
Row 132: 0, K2tog, K27
Row 133: 0, SK2tog, 0, K2tog, K7, MK, K3, MK, K7, SKtog, 0, K2tog, K1
Row 134: 0, K2tog, K25
Row 135: 0, SK2tog, 0, K2tog, K17, SKtog, 0, K2tog, K1
Row 136: 0, K2tog, K23
Row 137: 0, SK2tog, 0, K2tog, (K3, MK)3, K3, SKtog, 0, K2tog, K1
Row 138: 0, K2tog, K21
Row 139: 0, SK2tog, 0, K2tog, K13, SKtog, 0, K2tog, K1
Row 140: 0, K2tog, K19
Row 141: 0, SK2tog, 0, K2tog, (K3, MK)2, K3, SKtog, 0, K2tog, K1
Row 142: 0, K2tog, K17
Row 143: 0, SK2tog, 0, K2tog, K9, SKtog, 0, K2tog, K1
Row 144: 0, K2tog, K15
Row 145: 0, SK2tog, 0, K2tog, K3, MK, K3, SKtog, 0, K2tog, K1
Row 146: 0, K2tog, K13
Row 147: 0, SK2tog, 0, K2tog, K5, SKtog, 0, K2tog, K1
Row 148: 0, K2tog, K11
Row 149: 0, SK2tog, 0, K2tog, K3, SKtog, 0, K2tog, K1
Row 150: 0, K2tog, K9
Row 151: 0, SK2tog, 0, K2tog, K1, SKtog, 0, K2tog, K1
Row 152: 0, K2tog, K7
Row 153: 0, SK2tog, 0, SK2tog, 0, K2tog, K1
Row 154: 0, K2tog, K5
Row 155: 0, SK2tog, 0, SK2tog, K1
Row 156: 0, K2tog, K3
Row 157: 0, (K2tog)2, pso, K1
Row 158: 0, K2tog, K1
Row 159: SK2tog
Row 160: Fasten off

SMALL KNOB SQUARE TO MATCH CORINTHIAN PATTERN

Work the first 28 rows of the Corinthian pattern.
Continue as follows:

Row 29: 0, K2tog, 0, K5, (MK, K3)4, K2, 0, K2
Row 31: 0, K3tog, 0, K2tog, K19, SKtog, 0, K2tog, K1
Row 33: 0, K3tog, 0, K2tog, K4, (MK, K3)3, K1, SKtog, 0, K2tog, K1
Row 35: 0, K3tog, 0, K2tog, K15, SKtog, 0, K2tog, K1
Row 37: 0, K3tog, 0, K2tog, K4, (MK, K3)2, SKtog, 0, K2tog, K1
Row 39: 0, K3tog, 0, K2tog, K11, SKtog, 0, K2tog, K1
Row 41: 0, K3tog, 0, K2tog, K4, MK, K4, SKtog, 0, K2tog, K1
Row 43: 0, K3tog, 0, K2tog, K7, SKtog, 0, K2tog, K1
Row 45: 0, K3tog, 0, K2tog, K5, SKtog, 0, K2tog, K1
Row 47: 0, K3tog, 0, K2tog, K3, SKtog, 0, K2tog, K1
Row 49: 0, K3tog, 0, K2tog, K1, SKtog, 0, K2tog, K1
Row 51: 0, K3tog, 0, SK2tog, 0, K2tog, K1
Row 53: 0, K3tog, 0, SK2tog, K1
Row 55: 0, K2tog, K2tog, pso, K1
Row 57: SK2tog

Row 30: 0, K2tog, K27
Row 32: 0, K2tog, K25
Row 34: 0, K2tog, K23
Row 36: 0, K2tog, K21
Row 38: 0, K2tog, K19
Row 40: 0, K2tog, K17
Row 42: 0, K2tog, K15
Row 44: 0, K2tog, K13
Row 46: 0, K2tog, K11
Row 48: 0, K2tog, K9
Row 50: 0, K2tog, K7
Row 52: 0, K2tog, K5
Row 54: 0, K2tog, K3
Row 56: 0, K2tog, K1
Row 58: Fasten off

Work on a set of 5 needles
Each pattern is worked twice for each needle,
and 8 times for each round
Cast on 2 sts on each of 4 needles, and use the
fifth to knit. Knit 2 rounds plain.

Let X = 0, SKtog, 0

Round 1:	(0, K1)2	Round 2:	K4
Round 3:	(0, K2)2	Round 4:	K6
Round 5:	(X, K1)2	Round 6:	K8
Round 7:	X, P2, X, K2	Round 8:	K3, P2, K5
Round 9:	(X, K3)2	Round 10:	K12

Round 11: X, P4, X, K4	Round 12: K3, P4, K7
Round 13: (X, K5)2	Round 14: K16
Round 15: X, P6, X, K6	Round 16: K3, P6, K9
Round 17: (X, K7)2	Round 18: K20
Round 19: X, P8, X, K8	Round 20: K3, P8, K11
Round 21: (X, K9)2	Round 22: K24
Round 23: X, P10, X, K10	Round 24: K3, P10, K13
Round 25: (X, K11)2	Round 26: K28
Round 27: X, P12, X, K12	Round 28: K3, P12, K15
Round 29: (X, K13)2	Round 30: K32
Round 31: X, P14, X, K14	Round 32: K3, P14, K17
Round 33: (X, K15)2	Round 34: K36
Round 35: X, P16, X, K16	Round 36: K3, P16, K19
Round 37: (X, K17)2	Round 38: K40
Round 39: X, P18, X, K18	Round 40: K3, P18, K21
Round 41: (X, K19)2	Round 42: K44
Round 43: X, P20, X, K20	Round 44: K3, P20, K23

Round 45: Cast off 3 stitches, leaving 1 st on needle
K17, K2tog, turn and knit on these 19 sts.

Continue on 2 needles in short rows to slant off the ridged
knitting to a point of 1 stitch only. Slip the first stitch
on every row appropriately to make a neat edge. The pattern
is written for a single picot edge: start each row 0, K2tog

Row 1: P14, K2tog, K1	Row 2: P13, K2tog, K1
Row 3: K12, K2tog, K1	Row 4: K11, K2tog, K1
Row 5: P10, K2tog, K1	Row 6: P9, K2tog, K1
Row 7: K8, K2tog, K1	Row 8: K7, K2tog, K1
Row 9: P6, K2tog, K1	Row 10: P5, K2tog, K1
Row 11: K4, K2tog, K1	Row 12: K3, K2tog, K1
Row 13: P2, K2tog, K1	Row 14: P1, K2tog, K1
Row 15: K2tog, K1	Row 16: K2tog
Row 17: K1, pass st over	Row 18: K2tog and fasten off

Return to the place where you divided for the point, and, working
further along on the 45th round, cast off 26 stitches. Now
K17 over the purled stitches of the last round, K2tog and continue
on these 19 stitches as above, then cast off 26 stitches
along the round etc until a complete square is formed.

Knit 4 squares to form one lily.

The design looks most striking if the lily 'leaves' are grafted together when the squares are joined. Simply keep stitches in holding rather than casting them off. The section worked on 2 needles has been written for a single picot edge so that the whole square can conveniently be grafted after tensioning. If the square is starched as well as tensioned the open loops will not run.

The swirls made by knitting in rounds detract from the square shape; add a 'Fleur-de-lis' border to complete the lily theme of the quilt.

Complete Lily Pattern Square: Twilley's Handicraft No 1, 3.5 mm (10) needles:
54 cm (21") square took 250 gm (9 Oz) yarn

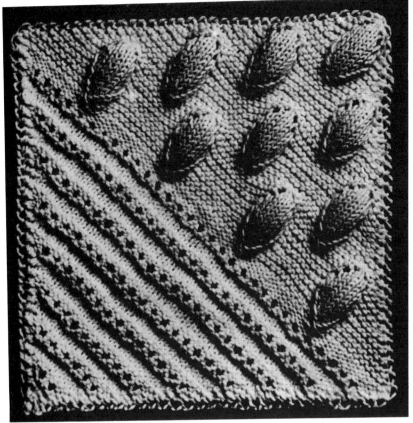

This pattern is attractive worked in two colours; the illustration on page 2 shows the pattern worked in a dark colour for the raised snowdrop part and a lighter colour used for the lace part. The original pattern instructions emphasize the ridges at the expense of the lace. I have adapted the pattern above to emphasize the lace, which then forms the ridges.

Each square took roughly three hours to knit. Twilley's Handicraft Cotton No 1 combined with 3.25 mm (10) needles produced a 25 cm (10") square, weighing 65 gm (2½ oz). Worked in a 4-ply synthetic yarn, on 2.5 mm (12) needles, the large pattern square composed of four small patterns measured 36 cm (14") square, and weighed 90 gm (3 0z). It's important to tension the shape properly to bring out the 'raised' snowdrops.

Work on a pair of needles
Cast on 1 stitch and (K1,P1,K1) into this stitch
Start each row with a single or double over

Row 1: K2tog, K1
Row 3: K2tog, K3
Row 5: K2tog, K1, P3, K3
Row 7: K2tog, K2, P5, K4
Row 9: K2tog, K3, P7, K5
Row 11: K2tog, K4, P9, K6
Row 13: K2tog, K5, P7, K7
Row 15: K2tog, K6, P5, K8
Row 17: K2tog, K7, P3, K9
Row 19: K2tog, K19
Row 21: K2tog, K2, P3, K13, P3, K4
Row 23: K2tog, K3, P5, K13, P5, K5
Row 25: K2tog, K4, P7, K13, P7, K6
Row 27: K2tog, K5, P9, K13, P9, K7

Row 2: K1, (K1,P1) in next st, K1
Row 4: K2, (0, K1)3
Row 6: (K3, 0)2, K2, 0, K1
Row 8: K4, 0, K5, 0, K3, 0, K1
Row 10: K5, 0, K7, 0, K4, 0, K1
Row 12: K6, SKtog, K5, K2tog, K5, 0, K1
Row 14: K7, SKtog, K3, K2tog, K6, 0, K1
Row 16: K8, SKtog, K1, K2tog, K7, 0, K1
Row 18: K9, SK2tog, K8, 0, K1
Row 20: K3, 0, K1, 0, K13, 0, K1, 0, K2, 0, K1
Row 22: K4, 0, K3, 0, K13, (0,K3)2, 0, K1
Row 24: (K5, 0)2, K13, 0, K5, 0, K4, 0, K1
Row 26: K6, 0, K7, 0, K13, 0, K7, 0, K5, 0, K1

Row 28: K7, SKtog, K5, K2tog, K13, SKtog, K5, K2tog, K6, 0, K1
Row 29: K2tog, K6, P7, K13, P7, K8
Row 30: K8, SKtog, K3, K2tog, K13, SKtog, K3, K2tog, K7, 0, K1
Row 31: K2tog, K7, P5, K13, P5, K9
Row 32: K9, SKtog, K1, K2tog, K13, SKtog, K1, K2tog, K8, 0, K1
Row 33: K2tog, K8, P3, K13, P3, K10
Row 34: K10, SK2tog, K13, SK2tog, K9, 0, K1
Row 35: K2tog, K35
Row 36: K4, (0, K1, 0, K13)2, 0, K1, 0, K3, 0, K1
Row 37: K2tog, K3, (P3, K13)2, P3, K5
Row 38: K5, (0, K3, 0, K13)2, 0, K3, 0, K4, 0, K1
Row 39: K2tog, K4, (P5, K13)2, P5, K6
Row 40: K6, (0, K5, 0, K13)2, (0, K5)2, 0, K1
Row 41: K2tog, K5, (P7, K13)2, P7, K7
Row 42: K7, (0, K7, 0, K13)2, 0, K7, 0, K6, 0, K1
Row 43: K2tog, K6, (P9, K13)2, P9, K8
Row 44: K8, SKtog, (K5, K2tog, K13, SKtog)2, K5, K2tog, K7, 0, K1
Row 45: K2tog, K7, (P7, K13)2, P7, K9
Row 46: K9, (SKtog, K3, K2tog, K13)2, SKtog, K3, K2tog, K8, 0, K1
Row 47: K2tog, K8, (P5, K13)2, P5, K10
Row 48: K10, (SKtog, K1, K2tog, K13)2, SKtog, K1, K2tog, K9, 0, K1
Row 49: K2tog, K9, (P3, K13)2, P3, K11
Row 50: K11, (SK2tog, K13)2, SK2tog, K10, 0, K1
Row 51: K2tog, K51
Row 52: K5, (0, K1, 0, K13)3, 0, K1, 0, K4, 0, K1
Row 53: K2tog, K4, P3, (K13, P3)3, K6
Row 54: K6, (0, K3, 0, K13)3, 0, K3, 0, K5, 0, K1
Row 55: K2tog, K5, P5, (K13, P5)3, K7
Row 56: K7, (0, K5, 0, K13)3, 0, K5, 0, K6, 0, K1
Row 57: K2tog, K6, P7, (K13, P7)3, K8
Row 58: K8, (0, K7, 0, K13)3, (0, K7)2, 0, K1
Row 59: K2tog, K7, P9, (K13, P9)3, K9
Row 60: K9, (SKtog, K5, K2tog, K13)3, SKtog, K5, K2tcg, K8, 0, K1
Row 61: K2tog, K8, P7, (K13, P7)3, K10
Row 62: K10, (SKtog, K3, K2tog, K13)3, SKtog, K3, K2tog, K9, 0, K1
Row 63: K2tog, K9, P5, (K13, P5)3, K11
Row 64: K11, (SKtog, K1, K2tog, K13)3, SKtog, K1, K2tog, K10, 0, K1
Row 65: K2tog, K10, P3, (K13, P3)3, K12
Row 66: K12, (SK2tog, K13)3, SK2tog, K11, 0, K1

Row 67: K2tog, K67   Row 68: K2tog, P67
Row 69: K3tog, K63, K2tog, K1   Row 70: K2tog, P64, K1

Line of Holes: Row 71: K3tog, K1, (0, K2tog)30, K2tog, K1

Row 72: K2tog, P62, K1   Row 73: K3tog, P59, K2tog, K1
Row 74: K2tog, K61   Row 75: K3tog, P57, K2tog, K1
Row 76: K2tog, K59   Row 77: K3tog, K55, K2tog, K1
Row 78: K2tog, P56, K1

Line of Holes: Row 79: K3tog, K1, (0, K2tog)26, K2tog, K1

Row 80: K2tog, P54, K1   Row 81: K3tog, P51, K2tog, K1
Row 82: K2tog, K53   Row 83: K3tog, P49, K2tog, K1
Row 84: K2tog, K51   Row 85: K3tog, K47, K2tog, K1
Row 86: K2tog, P48, K1

Line of Holes: Row 87: K3tog, K1, (0, K2tog)22, K2tog, K1

Row 88: K2tog, P46, K1   Row 89: K3tog, P43, K2tog, K1
Row 90: K2tog, K45   Row 91: K3tog, P41, K2tog, K1
Row 92: K2tog, K43   Row 93: K3tog, K39, K2tog, K1
Row 94: K2tog, P40, K1

Line of Holes: Row 95: K3tog, K1, (0, K2tog)18, K2tog, K1

Row 96: K2tog, P38, K1   Row 97: K3tog, P35, K2tog, K1
Row 98: K2tog, K37   Row 99: K3tog, P33, K2tog, K1
Row 100: K2tog, K35   Row 101: K3tog, K31, K2tog, K1
Row 102: K2tog, P32, K1

Line of Holes: Row 103: K3tog, K1, (0, K2tog)14, K2tog, K1

Row 104: K2tog, P30, K1   Row 105: K3tog, P27, K2tog, K1
Row 106: K2tog, K29   Row 107: K3tog, P25, K2tog, K1
Row 108: K2tog, K27   Row 109: K3tog, K23, K2tog, K1
Row 110: K2tog, P24, K1

Line of Holes: Row 111: K3tog, K1, (0, K2tog)10, K2tog, K1

Row 112: K2tog, P22, K1   Row 113: K3tog, P19, K2tog, K1
Row 114: K2tog, K21   Row 115: K3tog, P17, K2tog, K1
Row 116: K2tog, K19   Row 117: K3tog, K15, K2tog, K1
Row 118: K2tog, P16, K1

Line of Holes: Row 119: K3tog, K1, (0, K2tog)6, K2tog, K1

Row 120: K2tog, P14, K1   Row 121: K3tog, P11, K2tog, K1
Row 122: K2tog, K13   Row 123: K3tog, P9, K2tog, K1
Row 124: K2tog, K11   Row 125: K3tog, K7, K2tog, K1
Row 126: K2tog, P8, K1

Line of Holes: Row 127: K3tog, K1, (0, K2tog)2, K2tog, K1

Row 128: K2tog, P6, K1   Row 129: K3tog, P3, K2tog, K1
Row 130: K2tog, K5   Row 131: K3tog, P1, K2tog, K1
Row 132: K2tog, K3   Row 133: K3tog, K1; turn Sp, K2; turn SK2tog

Knit on a pair of needles
Cast on one stitch

The pattern is written for a double picot edge; this is quick
and easy to latch up.
Kbf means knit into the back and front of the stitch

Row 1: 02, Kbf	Row 2: 03, K2tog, 0, K1
Row 3: 02, K2tog, K1, Kbf	Row 4: 03, K2tog, K2, 0, K1
Row 5: 02, K2tog, K3, Kbf	Row 6: 03, K2tog, K4, 0, K1
Row 7: 02, K2tog, K5, Kbf	Row 8: 03, K2tog, K6, 0, K1
Row 9: 02, K2tog, K7, Kbf	Row 10: 03, K2tog, K8, 0, K1
Row 11: 02, K2tog, K9, Kbf	Row 12: 03, K2tog, K10, 0, K1
Row 13: 02, K2tog, K11, Kbf	Row 14: 03, K2tog, K12, 0, K1

Row 15: 02, K2tog, K13, Kbf	Row 16: 03, K2tog, K14, 0, K1
Row 17: 02, K2tog, K15, Kbf	Row 18: 03, K2tog, K16, 0, K1
Row 19: 02, K2tog, K17, Kbf	Row 20: 03, K2tog, (0,K2tog)9, 0, K1
Row 21: 02, K2tog, K19, Kbf	Row 22: 03, K2tog, (0,K2tog)10, 0, K1
Row 23: 02, K2tog, K21, Kbf	Row 24: 03, K2tog, P22, 0, K1
Row 25: 02, K2tog, K23, Kbf	Row 26: 03, K2tog, K24, 0, K1
Row 27: 02, K2tog, P25, Kbf	Row 28: 03, K2tog, K26, 0, K1
Row 29: 02, K2tog, K27, Kbf	Row 30: 03, K2tog, P28, 0, K1
Row 31: 02, K2tog, K29, Kbf	Row 32: 03, K2tog, P30, 0, K1
Row 33: 02, K2tog, P31, Kbf	Row 34: 02, K3tog, K29, K2tog, K1
Row 35: 02, K2tog, K31	Row 36: 02, K3tog, P27, P2tog, K1
Row 37: 02, K2tog, K29	Row 38: 02, K3tog, K25, K2tog, K1
Row 39: 02, K2tog, P26, K1	Row 40: 02, K3tog, K23, K2tog, K1
Row 41: 02, K2tog, K25	Row 42: 02, K3tog, P21, P2tog, K1
Row 43: 02, K2tog, K23	Row 44: 02, K3tog, (0,K2tog)10, K2tog
Row 45: 02, K2tog, K21	Row 46: 02, K3tog, (0,K2tog)9, K2tog
Row 47: 02, K2tog, K19	Row 48: 02, K3tog, K15, K2tog, K1
Row 49: 02, K2tog, K17	Row 50: 02, K3tog, K13, K2tog, K1
Row 51: 02, K2tog, K15	Row 52: 02, K3tog, K11, K2tog, K1
Row 53: 02, K2tog, K13	Row 54: 02, K3tog, K9, K2tog, K1
Row 55: 02, K2tog, K11	Row 56: 02, K3tog, K7, K2tog, K1
Row 57: 02, K2tog, K9	Row 58: 02, K3tog, K5, K2tog, K1
Row 59: 02, K2tog, K7	Row 60: 02, K3tog, K3, K2tog, K1
Row 61: 02, K2tog, K5	Row 62: 02, K3tog, K1, K2tog, K1
Row 63: 02, K2tog, K3	Row 64: 02, K3tog, K2tog
Row 65: 02, K2tog, K1	Row 66: K3tog

Fasten off.

Each square took approximately 40 minutes to knit. Knit 4 squares to make one large square. The photograph on page 57 shows 4 small squares connected by latch-up, and two sides edged with Armenian Lace. The lace is gathered at the corner by pulling 4 loops of the lace through 1 of the quilt selvedge, and repeating this 2 or 3 times just before and after the corner is reached.

Twilley's Stalite No 3, 2.75 mm (12) needles:
20 cm (8") square took 45 gm (1½ Oz) yarn

OPEN **S**HELL

Knit on a pair of needles
Cast on 57 stitches

Twilley's Handicraft No 1, 3.5 mm (10) needles:
20 cm (8") x 30 cm (12") took 28 gm (1 Oz) yarn

Start each row with (0, K2tog) to make a single picot edge

Row 1:	K55	Row 2:	K55
Row 3:	K55	Row 4:	K55
Row 5:	K55	Row 6:	K3, SKtog, K50
Row 7:	K3, SKtog, K49	Row 8:	K3, SKtog, K48
Row 9:	K3, P2tog, P42, K5	Row 10:	K3, SKtog, (0,K2tog)20, K6
Row 11:	K3, P2tog, P40, K5	Row 12:	K3, SKtog, K44
Row 13:	K3, P2tog, P38, K5	Row 14:	K3, P2tog, P37, K5
Row 15:	K3, K2tog, K41	Row 16:	K3, P2tog, P35, K5
Row 17:	K3, K2tog, K39	Row 18:	K3, SKtog, K38
Row 19:	K3, P2tog, P32, K5	Row 20:	K3, SKtog, (0,K2tog)15, K6
Row 21:	K3, P2tog, P30, K5	Row 22:	K3, SKtog, K34
Row 23:	K3, P2tog, P28, K5	Row 24:	K3, P2tog, P27, K5
Row 25:	K3, K2tog, K31	Row 26:	K3, P2tog, P25, K5
Row 27:	K3, K2tog, K29	Row 28:	K3, SKtog, K28

Row 29: K3, P2tog, P22, K5	Row 30: K3, SKtog, (0,K2tog)10, K6
Row 31: K3, P2tog, P20, K5	Row 32: K3, SKtog, K24
Row 33: K3, P2tog, P18, K5	Row 34: K3, P2tog, P17, K5
Row 35: K3, K2tog, K21	Row 36: K3, P2tog, P15, K5
Row 37: K3, K2tog, K19	Row 38: K3, K2tog, K18
Row 39: K3, P2tog, P12, K5	Row 40: K3, SKtog, (0,K2tog)5, K6
Row 41: K3, P2tog, P10, K5	Row 42: K3, SKtog, K14
Row 43: K3, P2tog, P8, K5	Row 44: K3, P2tog, P7, K5
Row 45: K3, K2tog, K11	Row 46: K3, P2tog, P5, K5
Row 47: K3, K2tog, K9	Row 48: K3, SKtog, K8
Row 49: K3, P2tog, P2, K5	Row 50: K3, SK2tog, K5
Row 51: K1, K2tog, K6	Row 52: K1, K2tog, K5
Row 53: K1, K2tog, K4	Row 54: K1, K2tog, K3
Row 55: (K2tog)2, K1	Row 56: K2tog, K1
Row 57: K2tog	Row 58: SKtog

Fasten off

The average knitting time for each pattern was one hour. This is a useful shape for setting between triangular quilt shapes which leave two edges of the quilt 'unfinished', as shown below. It is also a very useful shape to 'turn the corner' between two pieces of straight flouncing.

Work on a set of 4 needles
Cast on 37 stitches on each of 3 needles
Instructions given for EACH needle

Round 1: K
Round 2: K to last 2 sts, SKtog
Round 3: K to last 2 stitches, SKtog
Round 4: K to last 2 stitches, SKtog (34 stitches on each needle)
Round 5: Turn the work so that the last stitch of the third
          needle will now be the first stitch of the first
          needle, and, to prevent making a hole by turning,
          pass the under thread of the last stitch on the RHN
          on to the LHN, and knit it together with the last st;
          K to last 2 sts, SKtog

34

Round 6:   K to last 2 sts, SKtog
Round 7:   K to last 2 sts, SKtog
Round 8:   K to last 2 sts, SKtog (30 sts on each needle)

PATTERN REPEAT:
Repeat the instructions from Round 5 onwards; this will produce alternately raised and depressed 'ridges', with 4 rounds
forming each ridge.

The triangle formed by the 3 needles is decreased in this way
until 1 st remains on each needle. Break off the yarn, thread
through the remaining three stitches and pull up closely to
form a neat centre for the triangle. Knit 6 triangles to form
a hexagon shape.

Twilley's Handicraft No 1, 3.5 mm (10) needles:
21.5 cm (8") side equilateral triangle took 28 gm (1 Oz) yarn

The triangular pieces were first tensioned to form the 21.5 cm (8") side
triangles. Once tensioned, they were assembled by using oversew stitch,
working from the outside to the centre, and using white buttonhole thread
for strength without width. This produces an invisible join, forming a
subpattern of diamonds within the hexagon shape, which themselves form
a six-pointed star shape.

The hexagon was finished with
a small, reverse stocking
stitch square knitted on the
bias, pulled up into a roughly
circular button shape, and used
to fill the centre section.

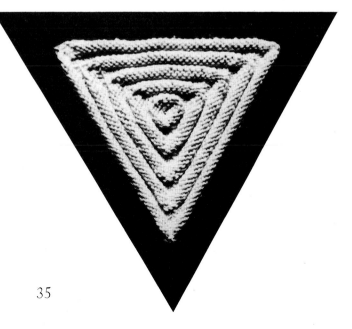

Knit on a pair of needles
Cast on 2 stitches

Falcon's thermacryl, 2.5 mm (12) needles:
36 cm (14") square took 60 gm (2 Oz) yarn

The pattern is written for a small picot edge; simply wind the yarn round the needle more than once for a larger picot edge.

(K1,P1,K1) means knit ALL THREE stitches into the next stitch

Leaf Pattern: Cast on 1 stitch and (K1,P1,K1)

Row 1: 0, K1, (K1,P1,K1), K1   Row 2: 0, K1, P3, K2
Row 3: 0, K3, 0, K1, 0, K3   Row 4: 0, K2, P5, K3
Row 5: 0, K5, 0, K1, 0, K5   Row 6: 0, K3, P7, K4

Row 7: 0, K7, 0, K1, 0, K7	Row 8: 0, K4, P9, K5
Row 9: 0, K9, 0, K1, 0, K9	Row 10: 0, K5, P11, K6
Row 11: 0, K11, 0, K1, 0, K11	Row 12: 0, K6, P13, K7
Row 13: 0, K13, 0, K1, 0, K13	Row 14: 0, K7, P15, K8
Row 15: 0, K15, 0, K1, 0, K15	Row 16: 0, K8, P17, K9
Row 17: 0, K9, SKtog, K13, K2tog, K9	Row 18: 0, K9, P15, K10
Row 19: 0, K10, SKtog, K11, K2tog, K10	Row 20: 0, K10, P13, K11
Row 21: 0, K11, SKtog, K9, K2tog, K11	Row 22: 0, K11, P11, K12
Row 23: 0, K12, SKtog, K7, K2tog, K12	Row 24: 0, K12, P9, K13
Row 25: 0, K13, SKtog, K5, K2tog, K13	Row 26: 0, K13, P7, K14
Row 27: 0, K14, SKtog, K3, K2tog, K14	Row 28: 0, K14, P5, K15
Row 29: 0, K15, SKtog, K1, K2tog, K15	Row 30: 0, K15, P3, K16
Row 31: 0, K16, SK2tog, K16	Row 32: 0, K16, P1, K17
Row 33: 0, K35	Row 34: 0, K36
Row 35: 0, K37	Row 36: 0, K1, P36, K1
Row 37: 0, K2, (0, K2tog)18, K1	Row 38: 0, K1, P38, K1
Row 39: 0, K41	Row 40: 0, K42
Row 41: 0, K1, P41, K1	Row 42: 0, K44
Row 43: 0, K45	Row 44: 0, K1, P44, K1

Diamond Pattern:

Row 45: 0, K2, (0, SK2tog, 0, K5)5, 0, SK2tog, 0, K2
Row 46: 0, K1, P46, K1
Row 47: 0, K1, K2tog, (0, K3, 0, SKtog, K1, K2tog)5, 0, K3, 0, SKtog, K1
Row 48: 0, K1, P48, K1
Row 49: 0, K1, K2tog, (0, K5, 0, SK2tog)5, 0, K5, 0, SKtog, K1
Row 50: 0, K1, P50, K1
Row 51: 0, K4, (0, SKtog, K1, K2tog, 0, K3)6, K1
Row 52: 0, K1, P52, K1
Row 53: 0, K6, (0, SK2tog, 0, K5)6, K1
Row 54: 0, K1, P54, K1

Row 55: 0, K57	Row 56: 0, K58
Row 57: 0, K1, P57, K1	Row 58: 0, K60
Row 59: 0, K61	Row 60: 0, K1, P60, K1
Row 61: 0, K2tog, (0, K2tog)30, K1	Row 62: 0, K1, P61, K1
Row 63: 0, K64	Row 64: 0, K65
Row 65: 0, K1, P64, K1	Row 66: 0, K67
Row 67: 0, K68	Row 68: 0, K1, P67, K1

Rows 69 - 87: Finish with the Spiral Pattern as given for the
'Group of Palm Leaves' pattern.

Work on a pair of needles
Cast on 2 stitches

Twilley's Lyscordet No 5, 2.75 mm (12) needles: 36 cm (14") square took 60 gm (2 Oz) yarn

The pattern is written for a small picot edge; simply wind the yarn round the needle more than once for a larger picot edge.

Pattern for the leaves: (K1,P1,K1) means knit ALL THREE in next st

Row 1: 0, K2	Row 2: 0, K3
Row 3: 0, K1, (K1,P1,K1), K2	Row 4: 0, K2, P3, K2
Row 5: 0, K3, 0, K1, 0, K4	Row 6: 0, K3, P5, K3
Row 7: 0, K5, 0, K1, 0, K6	Row 8: 0, K4, P7, K4
Row 9: 0, K7, 0, K1, 0, K8	Row 10: 0, K5, P9, K5
Row 11: 0, K9, 0, K1, 0, K10	Row 12: 0, K6, P11, K6

Row 13:   0, K11, 0, K1, 0, K12   Row 14:   0, K7, P13, K7
Row 15:   0, K13, 0, K1, 0, K14   Row 16:   0, K8, P15, K8
Row 17:   0, K3, (K1,P1,K1), K4, SKtog, K11, K2tog, K4, (K1,P1,K1), K4
Row 18:   0, K4, P3, K4, P13, K4, P3, K4
Row 19:   0, K5, 0, K1, 0, K5, SKtog, K9, K2tog, K5, 0, K1, 0, K6
Row 20:   0, K5, P5, K4, P11, K4, P5, K5
Row 21:   0, K7, 0, K1, 0, K6, SKtog, K7, K2tog, K6, 0, K1, 0, K8
Row 22:   0, K6,P7, K4, P9, K4, P7, K6
ROw 23:   0, K9, 0, K1, 0, K7, SKtog, K5, K2tog, K7, 0, K1, 0, K10
Row 24:   0, K7, P9, K4, P7, K4, P9, K7
Row 25:   0, K11, 0, K1, 0, K8, SKtog, K3, K2tog, K8, 0, K1, 0, K12
Row 26:   0, K8, P11, K4, P5, K4, P11, K8
Row 27:   0, K13, 0, K1, 0, K9, SKtog, K1, K2tog, K9, 0, K1, 0, K14
Row 28:   0, K9, P13, K4, P3, K4, P13, K9
Row 29:   0, K15, 0, K1, 0, K10, SK2tog, K10, 0, K1, 0, K16
Row 30:   0, K10, P15, K4, P1, K4, P15, K10
Row 31:   0, K10, SKtog, K11, K2tog, K4, (K1,P1,K1), K4, SKtog, K11,
          K2tog, K11
Row 32:   0, K11, P13, K4, P3, K4, P13, K11
Row 33:   0, K11, SKtog, K9, K2tog, K5, 0, K1, 0, K5, SKtog, K9, K2tog,
          K12
Row 34:   0, K12, P11, K4, P5, K4, P11, K12
Row 35:   0, K12, SKtog, K7, K2tog, K6, 0, K1, 0, K6, SKtog, K7, K2tog,
          K13
Row 36:   0, K13, P9, K4, P7, K4, P9, K13
Row 37:   0, K13, SKtog, K5, K2tog, K7, 0, K1, 0, K7, SKtog, K5,
          K2tog, K14
Row 38:   0, K14, P7, K4, P9, K4, P7, K14
Row 39:   0, K14, SKtog, K3, K2tog, K8, 0, K1, 0, K8, SKtog, K3,
          K2tog, K15
Row 40:   0, K15, P5, K4, P11, K4, P5, K15
Row 41:   0, K15, SKtog, K1, K2tog, K9, 0, K1, 0, K9, SKtog, K1,
          K2tog, K16
Row 42:   0, K16, P3, K4, P13, K4, P3, K16
Row 43:   0, K16, SK2tog, K10, 0, K1, 0, K10, SK2tog, K17
Row 44:   0, K22, P15, K22
Row 45:   0, K22, SKtog, K11, K2tog, K23
Row 46:   0, K23, P13, K23
Row 47:   0, K23, SKtog, K9, K2tog, K24
Row 48:   0, K24, P11, K24
Row 49:   0, K24, SKtog, K7, K2tog, K25
Row 50:   0, K25, P9, K25

Row 51:   0, K25, SKtog, K5, K2tog, K26   Row 52:   0, K26, P7, K26
Row 53:   0, K26, SKtog, K3, K2tog, K27   Row 54:   0, K27, P5, K27
Row 55:   0, K27, SKtog, K1, K2tog, K28   Row 56:   0, K28, P3, K28
Row 57:   0, K28, SK2tog, K29   Row 58:   0, K59
Row 59:   0, K60   Row 60:   0, K1, P59, K1
Row 61:   0, K2, (0, K2tog)29, K2   Row 62:   0, K1, P61, K1
Row 63:   0, K64   Row 64:   0, K65
Row 65:   0, K1, P64, K1   Row 66:   0, K67
Row 67:   0, K68   Row 68:   0, K1, P67, K1

Spiral pattern:

Row 69:   0, K2, (0, K1, SK2tog, K1, 0, K1)11, K2
Row 70:   0, K1, P69, K1
Row 71:   0, K3, (0, K1, SK2tog, K1, 0, K1)11, K3
Row 72:   0, K1, P71, K1
Row 73:   0, K4, (0, K1, SK2tog, K1, 0, K1)11, K4
Row 74:   0, K1, P73, K1
Row 75:   0, K5, (0, K1, SK2tog, K1, 0, K1)11, K5
Row 76:   0, K1, P75, K1
Row 77:   0, K6, (0, K1, SK2tog, K1, 0, K1)11, K6
Row 78:   0, K1, P77, K1
Row 79:   0, K7, (0, K1, SK2tog, K1, 0, K1)11, K7
Row 80:   0, K1, P79, K1
Row 81:   0, K8, (0, K1, SK2tog, K1, 0, K1)11, K8
Row 82:   0, K1, P81, K1
Row 83:   0, K9, (0, K1, SK2tog, K1, 0, K1)11, K9
Row 84:   0, K1, P83, K1
Row 85:   0, K86
Row 86:   0, K87
Row 87:   0, K1, P86, K1

Hold on needle for easy tensioning, or cast off purlwise. The open loops can be grafted to the open loops of another triangle.

This pattern can be combined with the 'Willow Leaf' pattern to form an unusual quilt. Each triangular 'Palm Leaves' piece took an average of $2\frac{1}{2}$ hours to knit; the 'Willow Leaf' took an average time of 2 hours. 4 triangles are needed to make a large square, and setting these together produces the attractive central pattern. The illustration shows the triangles assembled by using latch-up with a double picot edge.

This attractive square took an average knitting time of $2\frac{1}{2}$ hours; the instructions look more complicated than, in fact, they are. The pattern has been written out for a single picot edge.

As you can see from the illustration, the knitted up piece gives no idea of the 'dressed' look of the pattern. Neither the eyelet holes nor the 'blisters' are shown up until they are tensioned and starched into their pattern shapes.

Work on a pair of needles   Twilley's Lyscordet No 5, 2.75 mm (12) needles:
Cast on 2 stitches   36 cm (14") large square took 50 gm (2 Oz) yarn

(K, Kb) means knit into the front and back of the same stitch.

Let A = O, K2tog, K1
B B = K2tog, K3, O, K2tog, K3
   C = K4, O, K4

Row 1: (K, Kb)2
Row 3: O, K5
Row 5: O, K7
Row 7: A, K1, O, K4
Row 9: A, K1, O, K1, O, K4
Row 11: A, K1, O, K3, O, K4
Row 13: A, K1, O, K1, C
Row 15: A, K1, O, K3, C
Row 17: A, K1, O, K4, P1, C
Row 19: A, K1, O, K4, P3, C
Row 21: A, K1, O, K4, P5, C
Row 23: A, K1, O, K4, P3, O, K1, O, P3, C
Row 25: A, K1, O, K4, P4, O, K3, O, P4, C
Row 27: A, K1, O, K4, P5, O, K5, O, P5, C
Row 29: A, K1, O, K4, P6, K2, SK2tog, K2, P6, C
Row 30: A, K1, P5, K6, P5, K6, P5, K4
Row 31: A, K1, O, K4, P7, K1, SK2tog, K1, P7, C
Row 32: A, K1, P5, K7, P3, K7, P5, K4
Row 33: A, K1, O, K4, P3, O, K1, O, P4, SK2tog, P4, O, K1, O, P3, C
Row 34: A, K1, P5, K3, P3, K9, P3, K3, P5, K4
Row 35: A, K1, O, K4, P4, O, K3, O, P9, O, K3, O, P4, C
Row 36: A, K1, P5, K4, P5, K9, P5, K4, P5, K4
Row 37: A, K1, O, K4, P5, O, K5, O, P9, O, K5, O, P5, C
Row 38: A, K1, P5, K5, P7, K9, P7, K5, P5, K4
Row 39: A, K1, O, K4, P6, K2, SK2tog, K2, P9, K2, SK2tog, K2, P6, C
Row 40: A, K1, P5, K6, P5, K9, P5, K6, P5, K4
Row 41: A, K1, O, K4, P7, K1, SK2tog, K1, P4, O, P2tog, P3, K1, SK2tog, K1, P7, C
Row 42: A, K1, P5, K7, P3, K9, P3, K7, P5, K4
Row 43: A, K1, O, K4, P3, O, K1, O, P4, SK2tog, P3, O, P2tog, P1, O, P3, SK2tog, P4, O,
         K1, P3, C
Row 44: A, K1, P5, K3, P3, K20, P3, K3, P5, K4
Row 45: A, K1, O, K4, P4, O, K3, O, P7, O, P2tog, P1, O, P2tog, P1, O, P7, O, K3, O, P4, C
Row 46: A, K1, P5, K4, P5, K21, P5, K4, P5, K4
Row 47: A, K1, O, K4, P5, O, K5, O, P6, O, P2tog, K1, O, K2tog, K1, O, K2tog, K1, O,
         P6, O, K5, O, P5, C
Row 48: A, K1, P5, K5, P7, K22, P7, K5, P5, K4
Row 49: A, K1, O, K4, P6, K2, SK2tog, K2, P5, O, P2tog, P1, O, P2tog, P2, P2tog, O, P1,
         P2tog, O, P5, K2, SK2tog, K2, P6, C
Row 50: A, K1, P5, K6, P5, K22, P5, K6, P5, K4
Row 51: A, K1, O, K4, P7, K1, SK2tog, K1, P4, O, P2tog, P1, O, P2tog, P4, P2tog, O, P1,
         P2tog, O, P4, K1, SK2tog, K1, P7, C
Row 52: A, K1, P5, K7, P3, K22, P3, K7, P5, K4
Row 53: A, K1, O, K4, P3, O, K1, O, P4, SK2tog, P3, O, P2tog, P1, O, P2tog, P2, O, K2tog,
         O, P2, P2tog, O, P1, P2tog, O, P3, SK2tog, P4, O, K1, O, P3, C
Row 54: A, K1, P5, K3, P3, K15, P3, K15, P3, K3, P5, K4
Row 55: A, K1, O, K4, P4, O, K3, O, P7, O, P2tog, P1, O, P2tog, P3, O, K3, O, P3, P2tog,
         O, P1, P2tog, O, P7, O, K3, O, P4, C
Row 56: A, K1, P5, K4, P5, K15, P5, K15, P5, K4, P5, K4
Row 57: A, K1, O, K4, P5, O, K5, O, P6, O, P2tog, P1, O, P2tog, P4, O, K5, O, P4, P2tog,
         O, P1, P2tog, O, P6, O, K5, O, P5, C
Row 58: A, K1, P5, K5, P7, K15, P7, K15, P7, K5, P5, K4

Row 2: O, K4
Row 4: O, K6
Row 6: A, K5
Row 8: A, K1, P1, K4
Row 10: A, K1, P3, K4
Row 12: A, K1, P5, K4
Row 14: A, K1, P7, K4
Row 16: A, K1, P9, K4
Row 18: A, K1, P5, K1, P5, K4
Row 20: A, K1, P5, K3, P5, K4
Row 22: A, K1, P5, K5, P5, K4
Row 24: A, K1, P5, K3, P3, K3, P5, K4
Row 26: A, K1, P5, K4, P5, K4, P5, K4
Row 28: A, K1, P5, K5, P7, K5, P5, K4

42

Row 59: A, K2tog, O, K3, SKtog, P4, K2, SK2tog, K2, P5, P2tog, P1, O, P2tog, P1, O, P4, K2, SK2tog, K2, P4, O, P1, P2tog, O, P1, P2tog, P5, K2, SK2tog, K2, P4, B

Row 60: A, K1, P5, K4, P5, K15, P5, K15, P5, K4, P5, K4

Row 61: A, K2tog, O, K3, SKtog, P3, K1, SK2tog, K1, P6, P2tog, P1, O, P2tog, P1, O, P3, K1, SK2tog, K1, P3, O, P1, P2tog, O, P1, P2tog, P6, K1, SK2tog, K1, P3, B

Row 62: A, K1, P5, K3, P3, K15, P3, K15, P3, K3, P5, K4

Row 63: A, K2tog, O, K3, SKtog, P2, SK2tog, P4, O, K1, O, P2, P2tog, P1, O, P2tog, P1, O, P2, SK2tog, P2, O, P1, P2tog, O, P1, P2tog, P2, O, K1, O, P4, SK2tog, P2, B

Row 64: A, K1, P5, K7, P3, K10, (K1, P1), K10, P3, K7, P5, K4

Row 65: A, K2tog, O, K3, SKtog, P6, O, K3, O, P3, P2tog, P1, O, P2tog, P1, O, P4, O, P1, P2tog, O, P1, P2tog, P3, O, K3, O, P6, B

Row 66: A, K1, P5, K6, P5, K22, P5, K6, P5, K4

Row 67: A, K2tog, O, K3, SKtog, P5, O, K5, O, P4, P2tog, P1, O, P2tog, P1, O, P2, O, P1, P2tog, O, P1, P2tog, P4, O, K5, O, P5, B

Row 68: A, K1, P5, K5, P7, K22, P7, K5, P5, K4

Row 69: A, K2tog, O, K3, SKtog, P4, K2, SK2tog, K2, P5, P2tog, P1, O, P2tog, P1, O, P1, P2tog, O, P1, P2tog, P5, K2, SK2tog, K2, P4, B

Row 70: A, K1, P5, K4, P5, K21, P5, K4, P5, K4

Row 71: A, K2tog, O, K3, SKtog, P3, K1, SK2tog, K1, P6, P2tog, P1, O, P2tog, P1, O, P1, P2tog, P6, K1, SK2tog, K1, P3, B

Row 72: A, K1, P5, K3, P3, K20, P3, K3, P5, K4

Row 73: A, K2tog, O, K3, SKtog, P2, SK2tog, P4, O, K1, O, P2, P2tog, P1, O, P1, P2tog, P2, O, K1, O, P4, SK2tog, P2, B

Row 74: A, K1, P5, K7, P3, K9, P3, K7, P5, K4

Row 75: A, K2tog, O, K3, SKtog, P6, O, K3, O, P9, O, K3, O, P6, B

Row 76: A, K1, P5, K6, P5, K9, P5, K6, P5, K4

Row 77: A, K2tog, O, K3, SKtog, P5, O, K5, O, P9, O, K5, O, P5, B

Row 78: A, K1, P5, K5, P7, K9, P7, K5, P5, K4

Row 79: A, K2tog, O, K3, SKtog, P4, K2, SK2tog, K2, P9, K2, SK2tog, K2, P4, B

Row 80: A, K1, P5, K4, P5, K9, P5, K4, P5, K4

Row 81: A, K2tog, O, K3, SKtog, P3, K1, SK2tog, K1, P9, K1, SK2tog, K1, P3, B

Row 82: A, K1, P5, K3, P3, K9, P3, K3, P5, K4

Row 83: A, K2tog, O, K3, SKtog, P2, SK2tog, P4, O, K1, O, P4, SK2tog, P2

Row 84: A, K1, P5, K7, P3, K7, P5, K4

Row 85: A, K2tog, O, K3, SKtog, P6, O, K3, O, P6, B

Row 86: A, K1, P5, K6, P5, K6, P5, K4

Row 87: A, K2tog, O, K3, SKtog, P5, O, K5, O, P5, B

Row 88: A, K1, P5, K5, P7, K5, P5, K4

Row 89: A, K2tog, O, K3, SKtog, P4, K2, SK2tog, K2, P4, B

Row 90: A, K1, P5, K4, P5, K4, P5, K4

Row 91: A, K2tog, O, K3, SKtog, P3, K1, SK2tog, K1, P3, B

Row 92: A, K1, P5, K3, P3, K3, P5, K4

Row 93: A, K2tog, O, K3, SKtog, P2, SK2tog, P2, B

Row 94: A, K1, P5, K5, P5, K4

Row 95: A, K2tog, O, K3, SKtog, P3, B   Row 96: A, K1, P5, K3, P5, K4

Row 97: A, K2tog, O, K3, SKtog, P1, B   Row 98: A, K1, P5, K1, P5, K4

Row 99: A, K2tog, O, K3, SK2tog, K3, O, K2tog, K3

Row 100: A, K1, P9, K4

Row 101: A, K2tog, O, SKtog, K3, K2tog, O, K2tog, K3

Row 102: A, K1, P7, K4

Row 103: A, K2tog, O, SKtog, K1, K2tog, O, K2tog, K3

Row 104: A, K1, P5, K4

Row 105: A, K2tog, O, SK2tog, O, K2tog, K3   Row 106: A, K1, P3, K4

Row 107: A, K2tog, O, (K2tog)2, K2   Row 108: A, K1, P1, K4

Row 109: A, (K2tog)2, K2   Row 110: A, K4

Row 111: O, (K2tog)2, K3   Row 112: O, K2tog, K4

Row 113: O, (K2tog)3   Row 114: (K2tog)2, pso, fasten off

43

WEDGE PATTERN

Work on a pair of needles.
Cast on a multiple of 8 plus 3 edge stitches

Row 1: Sp, K4, *(P1, K7)*, P1, K5
Row 2: Sk, P4, *(K1, P7)*, K1, P5
Row 3: Sp, K3, *(P3, K5)*, P3, K4
Row 4: Sk, P3, *(K3, P5)*, K3, P4
Row 5: Sp, K2, *(P5, K3)*
Row 6: Sk, P2, *(K5, P3)*
Row 7: Sp, K1, *(P7, K1)*, K1
Row 8: Sk, P1, *(K7, P1)*, P1
Row 9: Sk, P1, *(K7, P1)*, K1
Row 10: Sp, K1, *(P7, K1)*, P1
Row 11: Sk, P2, *(K5, P3)*
Row 12: Sp, K2, *(P5, K3)*
Row 13: Sk, P3, *(K3, P5)*, K3, P4
Row 14: Sp, K3, *(P3, K5)*, P3, K4
Row 15: Sk, P4, *(K1, P7)*, K1, P5
Row 16: Sp, K4, *(P1, K7)*, P1, K5

PATTERN REPEAT:
Repeat rows 1 to 16.

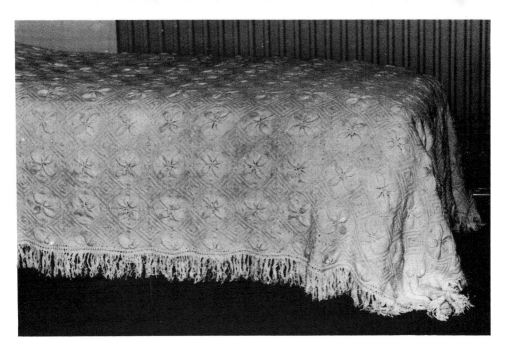

A 150 year old knitted quilt, made in heavy cotton. The quilt is borderd by a knotted fringe.
The detail below shows a corner of the quilt.

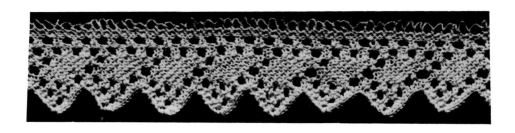

Knit on a pair of needles
Cast on 16 stitches and knit 1 row

Row 1: Sp, K2, (02, K2tog)2, K6, 02, K2tog, K1
Row 2: K3, P1, K8, P1, K2, P1, K3
Row 3: Sp, K18
Row 4: K
Row 5: Sp, K2, (02, K2tog)2, K7, (02, K2tog)2, K1
Row 6: K3, P1, K2, P1, K9, P1, K2, P1, K3
Row 7: Sp, K22
Row 8: K
Row 9: Sp, K2, (02, K2tog)2, (02, SK2tog)5, K1
Row 10: K3, P1, (K2, P1)6, K3
Row 11: Sp, K24
Row 12: C9, K15

PATTERN REPEAT:
Repeat rows 1 to 12

Twilley's Stalite No 3, 2.75 mm(12) needles:
60 cm (24") x 7.5 cm (3") took 25 gm (1 Oz) yarn

The pattern falls obliquely, matching well with garter or purl ridges worked on squares knitted from corner to corner. The average knitting time for one pattern repeat was 10 minutes.

F LEUR - DE - LIS E DGING

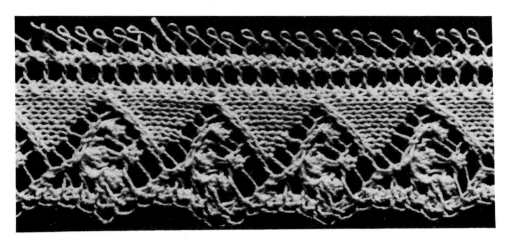

Work on a pair of needles
Cast on 14 stitches and knit 1 row

Row 1: Sp, K1, O, K2tog, K5, K2tog, O, K2tog, K1
Row 2: O, K2tog, O, P1, O, P2tog, P4, K4
Row 3: Sp, K1, O, K2tog, K3, K2tog, O, K3, O, K2
Row 4: O, K2tog, O, P1, O, P3tog, O, P1, O, P2tog, P2, K4
Row 5: Sp, K1, O, K2tog, K1, K2tog, O, K3, O, K1, O, K3, O, K2
Row 6: O, K2tog, P1, P3tog, O, P3, O, P3tog, P1, O, P2tog, K4
Row 7: Sp, K1, O, K2tog, K2, O, SK2tog, O, K3, O, SK2tog, O, K2
Row 8: O, K2tog, P2tog, P1, P3tog, P2tog, O, P3, K4
Row 9: Sp, K1, O, K2tog, K4, O, SK3tog, O, K2
Row 10: O, K2tog, P2tog, O, P5, K4
Row 11: Sp, K1, O, K2tog, K6, O, K1, O, K2
Row 12: O, K2tog, P2tog, P7, K4

PATTERN REPEAT:
Repeat rows 1 to 12

Twilley's Lyscordet No 5, 2.5 mm (12) needles:
60 cm (24") x 5 cm (2") took 20 gm (1 Oz) yarn

Each pattern repeat took an average of 6 minutes to knit. This most
attractive and unusual pattern can be used with either side as the
right side. It makes a suitable edging for the 'Lily' pattern, but needs
to be gathered at the corner to provide sufficient outside length to
lie flat.

Work on a pair of needles
Cast on 18 stitches

Single picot edge:

Row 1: O, K2tog, P11, K5	Row 2: K
Row 3: O, K2tog, P11, K5	Row 4: K5, P11, K2
Row 5: O, K2tog, K16	Row 6: K5, P11, K2
Row 7: O, K2tog, K16	Row 8: K5, P11, K2
Row 9: O, K2tog, (P1,Sp)5, P1, K5	Row 10: K5, (P1, K1)6, K1
Row 11: O, K2tog, K16	Row 12: K5, P11, K2
Row 13: O, K2tog, K16	Row 14: K5, P11, K2

Repeat rows 1 to 14 until the corner is reached.

Corner:

Row 1:	0, K2tog, P11, K5	Row 2:	K16, U:P11, K5	
Row 3:	K5, P10, U:Sp, K14	Row 4:	K5, P9, U:Sp, K13	
Row 5:	K5, P8, U:(P1,Sp)4, K5	Row 6:	K5, (P1,K1)3, P1, U:Sp, K11	
Row 7:	K5, U:Sp, K4	Row 8:	K5, P6, U:Sp, K10	
Row 9:	K5, U:Sp, K4	Row 10:	K5, P5, U:Sk, P4, K5	
Row 11:	K5, U:Sp, K4	Row 12:	K9, U:Sk, P3, K5	
Row 13:	K5, U:Sp, K4	Row 14:	K5, P3, U:Sp, K7	
Row 15:	K5, U:Sp, K4	Row 16:	K5, P2, U:Sp, K6	
Row 17:	K5, U:Sp, K4	Row 18:	K5, P1, U:Sp, K5	
Row 19:	K5, U:Sp, K4,			
	U:K5			
	U:Sp, K4	Row 20:	K6, U:Sp, K5	
Row 21:	K5, U:Sp, K4	Row 22:	K7, U:Sk, P1, K5	
Row 23:	K5, U:Sp, K4	Row 24:	K5, P3, U:Sp, K7	
Row 25:	K5, U:Sp, K4	Row 26:	K9, U:Sk, P3, K5	
Row 27:	K5, U:Sp, K4	Row 28:	K10, U:Sp, K9	
Row 29:	K5, U:Sp, K4	Row 30:	K5, P6, U:Sp, K10	
Row 31:	K5, U:Sp, K4	Row 32:	K5, P7, U:(P1,Sp)3, P1, K5	
Row 33:	K5, (P1,K1)4, U:Sp, K12	Row 34:	K5, P9, U:Sp, K13	
Row 35:	K5, P10, U:Sk, P9, K5	Row 36:	K16, U:Sk, P10, K5	
Row 37:	K5, P11, K2			

Continue the straight part of the fringe, starting with Row 5.
Twilley's Stalite No 3, 2.75 mm (12) needles: 90 cm (35") including corner x 10 cm (4")
took 50 gm (2 Oz) yarn

The average knitting time for the 14 row repeat was 8 minutes. The fringe
is made by dropping the last 3 stitches on the end opposite the picots,
and pulling out the long loops. Graft the two straight ends together after
the fourth corner. The fringe loops will have kinks from the knitting;
they can readily be straightened out by wetting and starching the loops,
and pulling them taut by inserting a knitting needle or ruler through them.

This pattern is a neat and simple finish for any quilt; the easily turned
corner gives it a professional finish.

Work on a pair of needles
Cast on 16 stitches

Let A = Sp, K2tog, O2, K2tog, K1

Foundation row: K5, P5, K6

Row 1: A, (P1, Sp)2, P1, 0, P5;
U:K5, U:P5

Row 2: P11, K3, P1, K2

Row 3: Sp, K5, (Sp,P1)3, 0, K5;
U:P5, U:K5

Row 4: K5, P7, K6

Row 5: A, (P1,Sp)3, P1, 0, P5;
U:K5, U:P5

Row 6: P13, K3, P1, K2

Row 7: Sp, K5, (Sp, P1)4, 0, K5;
U:P5, U:K5

Row 8: K5, P9, K6

Row 9: A, (P1, Sp)4, P1, 0, P5;
U:K5, U:P5

Row 10: P15, K3, P1, K2

Row 11: Sp, K5, (Sp, P1)5, 0, K5;
U:P5, U:K5

Row 12: K5, P11, K6

Row 13: A, (P1,Sp)5, P1, O, P5;
         U:K5, U:P5

Row 14: P17, K3, P1, K2

Row 15: Sp, K5, (Sp,P1)6, O, K5;
         U:P5, U:K5

Row 16: K5, P13, K6

Row 17: A, (P1,Sp)6, P1, O, P5;
         U:K5, U:P5

Row 18: P19, K3, P1, K2

Row 19: Sp, K5, (Sp,P1)7, O, K5;
         U:P5, U:K5

Row 20: K5, P15, K6

Row 21: A, (P1,Sp)7, P1, O, P5;
         U:K5, U:P5

Row 22: P21, K3, P1, K2

Row 23: Sp, K5, (Sp,P1)8, O, K5;
         U:P5, U:K5

Row 24: K5, P17, K6

Row 25: A, (P1,Sp)8, P1, O, P5;
         U:K5, U:P5

Row 26: P23, K3, P1, K2

Row 27: Sp, K5, (Sp,P1)9, O, K5;
         U:P5, U:K5

Row 28: K5, P19, K6

Row 29: A, (P1,Sp)9, P1, O, P5;
         U:K5, U:P5

Row 30: P25, K3, P1, K2

Row 31: Sp, K5, (Sp,P1)10, O, K5;
         U:P5, U:K5

Row 32: K5, P1, P3tog, P17, K6

Row 33: A, (P1,Sp)9, P1, O, P5;
         U:K5, U:P5

Row 34: P6, P3tog, P16, K3, P1, K2

Row 35: Sp, K5, (Sp,P1)9, O, K5;
         U:P5, U:K5

Row 36: K5, P1, P3tog, P15, K6

Row 37: A, (P1,Sp)8, P1, O, P5;
         U:K5, U:P5

Row 38: P6, P3tog, P14, K3, P1, K2

Row 39: Sp, K5, (Sp,P1)8, O, K5;
         U:P5, U:K5

Row 40: K5, P1, P3tog, P13, K6

Row 41: A, (P1,Sp)7, P1, O, P5;
         U:K5, U:P5

Row 42: P6, P3tog, P12, K3, P1, K2

Row 43: Sp, K5, (Sp,P1)7, O, K5;
         U:P5, U:K5

Row 44: K5, P1, P3tog, P11, K6

Row 45: A, (P1,Sp)6, P1, O, P5;
         U:K5, U:P5

Row 46: P6, P3tog, P10, K3, P1, K2

Row 47: Sp, K5, (Sp,P1)6, O, K5;
         U:P5, U:K5

Row 48: K5, P1, P3tog, P9, K6

Row 49: A, (P1,Sp)5, P1, O, P5;
         U:K5, U:P5

Row 50: P6, P3tog, P8, K3, P1, K2

Row 51: Sp, K5, (Sp,P1)5, O, K5;
         U:P5, U:K5

Row 52: K5, P1, P3tog, P7, K6

Row 53: A, (P1,Sp)4, P1, O, P5;
         U:K5, U:P5

Row 54: P6, P3tog, P6, K3, P1, K2

Row 55: Sp, K5, (Sp,P1)4, 0, K5;   Row 56: K5, P1, P3tog, P5, K6
         U:P5, U:K5
Row 57: A, (P1,Sp)3, P1, 0, P5;   Row 58: P6, P3tog, P4, K3, P1, K2
         U:K5, U:P5
Row 59: Sp, K5, (Sp,P1)3, 0, K5;   Row 60: K5, P1, P3tog, P3, K6
         U:P5, U:K5

PATTERN REPEAT: Twilley's Stalite No 3, 2.75 mm (12) needles:
Repeat rows 1 to 60   33 cm (13") x 10 cm (4") took 25 gm (1 Oz) yarn

Each set of 60 rows took an average knitting time of 50 minutes. This is a particularly attractive flounce for a quilt; the knitted-in ruffle on the vandyke edge is an unusual feature which is readily made by knitting 2 extra rows on 5 stitches only every other row.

The flounce is recommended for ornamenting a reticule, that is a lady's pocket or work bag, and also for sash ends. A sash was a scarf worn round the waist, or sometimes with one end over the shoulder, and was generally finished in a fringe or flounce.

Four 'Mulberry-Leaf' squares joined with latch-up. A mother-of-pearl button adds interest.

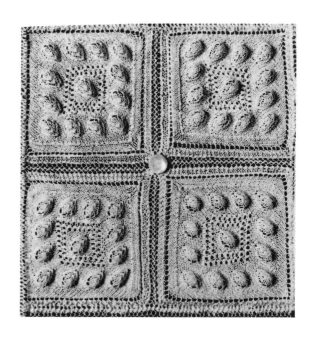

VALENCIENNES BORDER

Knit on a pair of needles
Cast on 26 stitches and knit 1 row

Row 1: K2tog, K1, O, K2tog, K5, K2tog, O, K2tog, K9, O, K2tog, K1
Row 2: Sp, K2, O, K2tog, K1, (K2tog, O)2, K2tog, K2, O, K2tog,
         K3, K2tog, O, K3
Row 3: O, K4, O, K2tog, K1, K2tog, O, K11, O, K2tog, K1
Row 4: Sp, K2, O, K2tog, K3, (O, K2tog)2, K3, O, K3tog, O, K6
Row 5: O, K1, K2tog, O2, K18, O, K2tog, K1
Row 6: Sp, K2, O, K2tog, K4, (O, K2tog)2, K9, P1, K3
Row 7: K1, K2tog, (O2, K2tog)2, K16, O, K2tog, K1
Row 8: Sp, K2, O, K2tog, K5, (O, K2tog)2, K7, (P1, K2)2
Row 9: K2tog, K1, K2tog, O2, K2tog, K3, O, K1, O, K2tog, K11,
         O, K2tog, K1
Row 10: Sp, K2, O, K2tog, K3, K2tog, O, K2tog, (O, K3)2, O,
         K2tog, K3, P1, K2tog, K1
Row 11: K2tog, K3, K2tog, O, K5, O, K2tog, K10, O, K2tog, K1
Row 12: Sp, K2, O, K2tog, K2, (K2tog, O)2, K3, O, K7, O, K2tog,
         K1, K2tog

PATTERN REPEAT:
Repeat rows 1 to 12.

Twilley's Lyscordet No 5, 2.5 mm (12) needles:
60 cm (24") x 10 cm (4") took 25 gm (1 Oz) yarn

Average knitting time for each pattern repeat was 12 minutes

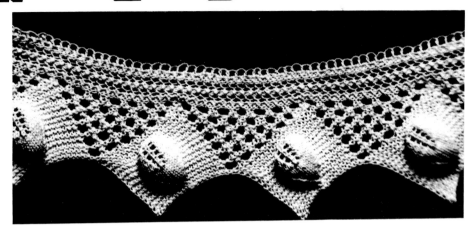

Knit on a pair of needles
Cast on 30 sts and knit 1 row

Let A = Sp, K3, (0, K2tog, K1)2
    B = K3, (0, K2tog, K1)2, K1

Row 1: A, 02, K2tog, K18
Row 2: Sp, K8, (K1,P1,K1) all in next st, K10, P1, B
Row 3: A, K11, P3, K9
Row 4: Sp, K9, 0, K1, 0, K12, B
Row 5: A, (02, K2tog,)2, K7, P5, K9
Row 6: Sp, K10, 0, K1, 0, K11, P1, K2, P1, B
Row 7: A, K13, P7, K9
Row 8: Sp, K11, 0, K1, 0, K16, B
Row 9: A, (02, K2tog)3, K7, P9, K9
Row 10: Sp, K12, 0, K1, 0, K13, (P1, K2)2, P1, B
Row 11: A, K16, P11, K9
Row 12: Sp, K13, 0, K1, 0, K21, B
Row 13: A, (02, K2tog)2, 02, SK2tog, 02, K2tog, K7, P13, K9
Row 14: Sp, K8, SKtog, K9, K2tog, K9, (P1, K2)3, P1, B
Row 15: A, K19, P11, K9
Row 16: Sp, K8, SKtog, K7, K2tog, K19, B
Row 17: A, (02, K2tog)2, (02, SK2tog)2, 02, K2tog, K7, P9, K9
Row 18: Sp, K8, SKtog, K5, K2tog, K9, (P1, K2)4, P1, B
Row 19: A, K22, P7, K9
Row 20: Sp, K8, SKtog, K3, K2tog, K22, B

Row 21: A, (02, K2tog)2, (02, SK2tog)3, 02, K2tog, K7, P5, K9
Row 22: Sp, K8, SKtog, K1, K2tog, K9, (P1, K2)5, P1, B
Row 23: A, K25, P3, K9
Row 24: Sp, K8, SK2tog, K25, B
Row 25: A, (02, K2tog)2, (02, SK2tog)4, 02, K2tog, K17
Row 26: Sp, K18, P1, (K2, P1)6, B
Row 27: A, K38
Row 28: C18, K19, B

PATTERN REPEAT:
Repeat rows 1 to 28.

Twilley's Stalite No 3, 2.5 mm (12) needles:
55 cm (21") x 12 cm (5") took 40 gm (1½ Oz) yarn

The average hand knitting time for each pattern repeat was 40 minutes.

Any quilt with similar raised leaves in the pattern is conveniently finished with this delightful border. The pattern also fits well with any other type of embossed quilt pattern.

Small 'Corinthian' corner square between two flounces

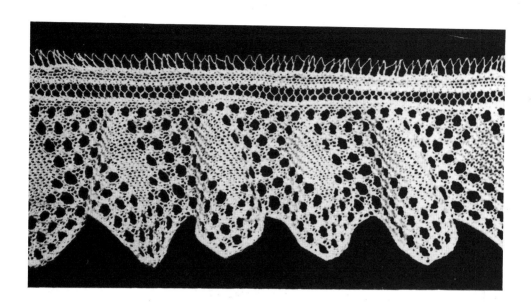

Work on a pair of needles
Cast on 28 stitches and knit 1 row

Let A = Sp, K4, 0, K2tog
    B = K3, 0, K2tog, K3

Row 1:   A, K1, 02, K2tog, K11, (02, K2tog)3, K1
Row 2:   Sp, (K2, P1)3, K13, P1. B
Row 3:   A, K25
Row 4:   Sp, K23, B
Row 5:   A, K1, (02, K2tog)2, K13, (02, K2tog)3, K1
Row 6:   Sp, (K2, P1)3, K15, P1, K2, P1, B
Row 7:   A, K30
Row 8:   Sp, K28, B
Row 9:   A, K1, (02, K2tog)3, K16, (02, K2tog)3, K1
Row 10:   Sp, (K2, P1)3, K18, (P1, K2)2, P1, B
Row 11:   A, K36
Row 12:   Sp, K34, B
Row 13:   A, K1, 02, K2tog, (02, K3tog)10, 02, K2tog, K1
Row 14:   Sp, (K2, P1)12, B

Row 15: A, K38
Row 16: Sp, K36, B
Row 17: A, K1, (02, K3tog)12, K1
Row 18: Sp, (K2, P1)12, B
Row 19: A, K38
Row 20: Sp, K36, B
Row 21: A, K1, (02, K3tog)12, K1
Row 22: Sp, (K2, P1)12, B
Row 23: A, K38
Row 24: C17, K19, B

PATTERN REPEAT:
Repeat rows 1 to 24

Twilley's Lyscordet No 5, 2.5 mm (12) needles:
45 cm (17½") x 14 cm (5½") took 25 gm (1 0z) yarn

The average knitting time for each pattern repeat was 30 minutes.

'Open Ribbed' pattern bordered by 'Armenian' lace

I VY P ATTERN

Work on a pair of needles
Cast on 18 stitches

Let A = 0, K2tog, K1
    B = 0, (K2tog)2
  pso = slip 1st K2tog over 2nd K2tog, thus decreasing 1 stitch

Row 1:   0, K17, P1
Row 2:   P1, K2tog, O2, K2tog, K11, A
Row 3:   0, K14, P2, K1, P2
Row 4:   P1, K7, (0, K1)4 in next st, K5, K2tog, 0, K1, A
Row 5:   0, K11, P8, K3, P5
Row 6:   P1, K2tog, O2, K2tog, K3, (K2tog, K4)2, K2tog, 0, K3, A
Row 7:   0, K12, P6, K3, P2, K1, P2
Row 8:   P1, K7, K2tog, K2, K2tog, K3, K2tog, 0, K5, A
Row 9:   0, K13, P4, K3, P5
Row 10:   P1, K2tog, O2, K2tog, K3, (K2tog)2, pso, K2, K2tog, 0, K3,
          (0, K1)4 in next st, K3, A
Row 11:   0, K6, P8, K11, P2, K1, P2
Row 12:   P1, K5, 0, K2tog, K2, K2tog, 0, K4, (K2tog, K4)2, A
Row 13:   0, K7, P6, K9, P1, K1, P5

58

Row 14: P1, K2tog, O2, K2tog, (O, K2tog)2, K2tog, O, K3,
(O, K1)4 in next st, K1, K2tog, K2, K2tog, K1,
(O, K1)4 in next st, K3, A
Row 15: O, K6, P8, K1, P4, K1, P8, K6, P5, K1, P2
Row 16: P1, K5, O, (K2tog)2, O, (K4, K2tog)2, K1, (K2tog)2,
pso, K1, (K2tog, K4)2, A
Row 17: O, K7, P6, K3, P6, K7, P7
Row 18: P1, K2tog, O2, K2tog, K2, O, K2tog, K1, O, (K2tog, K2)2,
K2tog, K1, (O, K1)4 in next st, K1, K2tog, (K2, K2tog)2, B
Row 19: O, K6, P4, K1, P8, K1, P4, K6, P1, K1, P3, K1, P2
Row 20: P1, K5, (O, K2tog)2, K1, O, K2tog, K1, (K2tog)2, pso, K1,
K2tog, K4, K2tog, K1, (K2tog)2, pso, K1, K2tog, B
Row 21: O, K7, P6, K7, P3, K1, P5
Row 22: P1, K2tog, O2, K2tog, K2, O, K2tog, K3, O, K2tog,
(K2, K2tog)3, B
Row 23: O, K6, P4, K8, P1, K1, P3, K1, P2
Row 24: P1, K7, (O, K1)4 in next st, K4, O, K2tog, K1, (K2tog)2,
pso, K1, K2tog, B
Row 25: O, K13, P8, K3, P5
Row 26: P1, K2tog, O2, K2tog, K3, (K2tog, K4)2, K1, O, K2tog, K1,
K2tog, B
Row 27: O, K12, P6, K3, P2, K1, P2
Row 28: P1, K7, (K2tog, K2)2, K4, O, K3tog, B
Row 29: O, K11, P4, K3, P5
Row 30: P1, K2tog, O2, K2tog, K3, (K2tog)2, pso, K7, O, K3tog, K2tog
Row 31: O, K14, P2, K1, P2
Row 32: P1, K16, K3tog

PATTERN REPEAT:
Repeat rows 1 to 32

Twilley's Handicraft No 1, 3.25 mm (10) needles:
30 cm (12") x 14 cm (5½") took 30 gm (1 Oz) yarn

This pattern fits well with any quilt assembled from pieces having
relatively small embossed shapes, such as the 'Corinthian' pattern.
Small, round-headed buttons are useful for bringing out the shape of
the embossed 'Ivy' leaves.

A double picot edge, shown in the illustration, is useful for attaching
this border by latch-up.

Work on a pair of needles
Cast on 53 stitches and knit 1 row

Let A = K2tog, 02, K2tog; (Kb,K) means knit into back and front of st

Row 1: Sp, K1, A, K5, A, K7, A, K1, (0, K2tog)7, K3, A2, K1
Row 2: (K3, P1)2, K21, P1, K10, P1, K8, P1, K3
Row 3: Sp, K8, A2, K8, K2tog, (0, K2tog)5, 0, K4, A, K7, (Kb,K)
Row 4: K11, P1, K27, P1, K3, P1, K10
Row 5: Sp, K1, A, K5, A, K5, A, K2tog, (0, K2tog)5, 0, K2, A, K7, A, K1
Row 6: K3, P1, K10, P1, K17, (P1, K8)2, P1, K3
Row 7: Sp, K22, K2tog, (0, K2tog)4, 0, K2, A, K14, (Kb,K)
Row 8: K18, P1, K36
Row 9: Sp, K1, A, K12, A, K2tog, (0, K2tog)3, 0, K2, A, K14, A, K1

Row 10:   K3, P1, K17, P1, K13, P1, K15, P1, K3
Row 11:   Sp, K14, A, K2, K2tog, (0, K2tog)2, 0, K2, A, K21, (Kb,K)
Row 12:   K25, P1, K13, P1, K16
Row 13:   Sp, K1, A, K6, A, K4, (K2tog, 0)2, K2, A, K10, A, K7, A, K1
Row 14:   K3, P1, K10, P1, (K13, P1)2, K9, P1, K3
Row 15:   Sp, K8, A, K6, K2tog, 0, K2, A, K11, A2, K9, (Kb,K)
Row 16:   K13, P1, K3, P1, K14, P1, K13, P1, K10
Row 17:   Sp, K1, A2, K8, K2tog, 0, A, K16, A, K8, A, K1
Row 18:   K3, P1, K11, P1, K19, P1, K13, P1, K3, P1, K3
Row 19:   Sp, K8, A, K7, 0, K2tog, K1, A, K11, A2, K11
Row 20:   K13, P1, K3, P1, K14, P1, K13, P1, K10
Row 21:   Sp, K1, A, K6, A, K5, (0, K2tog)2, K1, A, K10, A, K7, A, K2tog
Row 22:   K3, P1, K10, P1, (K13, P1)2, K9, P1, K3
Row 23:   Sp, K14, A, K3, (0, K2tog)3, K1, A, K21, K2tog
Row 24:   K24, P1, K13, P1, K16
Row 25:   Sp, K1, A, K12, A, K1, (0, K2tog)4, K1, A, K14, A, K1
Row 26:   K3, P1, K17, P1, K13, P1, K15, P1, K3
Row 27:   Sp, K23, (0, K2tog)5, K1, A, K14, K2tog
Row 28:   K17, P1, K36
Row 29:   Sp, K1, A, K5, A, K5, A, K1, (0, K2tog)6, K1, A, K7, A, K1
Row 30:   K3, P1, K10, P1, K17, (P1, K8)2, P1, K3
Row 31:   Sp, K8, A2, K9, (0, K2tog)6, K3, A, K7, K2tog
Row 32:   K10, P1, K27, P1, K3, P1, K10
Row 33:   Sp, K1, A, K5, A, K7, A, K1, (0, K2tog)7, K3, A2, K1
Row 34:   (K3, P1)2, K21, P1, K10, P1, K8, P1, K3

PATTERN REPEAT:
Repeat rows 3 to 34

Twilley's Stalite No 3, 2.5 mm (12) needles:
55 cm (21") x 23 cm (9") took 75 gm (3 Oz) yarn

Each pattern repeat took an average of 1 hour to knit. Though the even rows look as though they form part of a complicated pattern, they merely indicate that the rows are knitted, except for a (K1, P1) in the double overs (02) of the previous row.

Replace the Sp, K1 at the beginning of the odd rows by (0, K2tog) or (02, K2tog) for single or double picot loops at the straight edge; the lace can then be joined neatly and easily to a similarly finished quilt edge.

𝕎 IDE 𝕙 ANDSOME 𝔹 ORDER

Work on a pair of needles
Cast on 36 stitches
Knit 1 row

Twilley's Lyscordet No 5, 2.5 mm (12) needles:
46 cm (18") x 18 cm (7") took 25 gm (1 Oz) yarn

Let A = K2tog, 02, K2tog
The double over (02) at the end of the odd rows is always treated as
a single over on the return row, and the second loop dropped.

Row 1: Sp, K3, 0, K2tog, K10, 0, K2tog, K11, K2tog, 0, K2, 02,
         K2tog, K1
Row 2: 0, K2tog, K18, 0, K2tog, K10, 0, K2tog, K2
Row 3: Sp, K3, 0, K2tog, K2, A, K4, 0, K2tog, K10, K2tog, 0, K4, 02, K2
Row 4: 0, K2tog, K19, 0, K2tog, K4, P1, K5, o, K2tog, K2
Row 5: Sp, K3, 0, K2tog, A2, K2, 0, K2tog, K9, K2tog, 0, K6, 02, K2
Row 6: 0, K2tog, K20, 0, K2tog, K2, P1, K3, P1, K3, 0, K2tog, K2
Row 7: Sp, K3, 0, K2tog, K2, A, K4, 0, K2tog, K8, K2tog, 0, K2, A,
         K2, 02, K2
Row 8: 0, K2tog, K5, P1, K15, 0, K2tog, K4, P1, K5, 0, K2tog, K2
Row 9: Sp, K3, 0, K2tog, A2, K2, 0, K2tog, K7, K2tog, 0, K1, A2,
         K1, 02, K2
Row 10: 0, K2tog, K4, P1, K3, P1, K13, 0, K2tog, K2, (P1,K3)2, 0, K2tog, K2

62

Row 11: Sp, K3, O, K2tog, K2, A, K4, O, K2tog, K6, K2tog, O, K4, A,
         K4, O2, K2
Row 12: O, K2tog, K7, P1, K15, O, K2tog, K4, P1, K5, O, K2tog, K2
Row 13: Sp, K3, O, K2tog, K10, O, K2tog, K5, K2tog, O, K3, A2, K3, O2, K2
Row 14: O, K2tog, K6, P1, K3, P1, K13, O, K2tog, K10, O, K2tog, K2
Row 15: Sp, K3, O, K2tog, K10, O, K2tog, K4, K2tog, O, K6, A, K6, O2, K2
Row 16: O, K2tog, K9, P1, K15, O, K2tog, K10, O, K2tog, K2
Row 17: Sp, K3, O, K2tog, K2, A, K4, O, K2tog, K3, K2tog, O, K2, A,
         K6, A, K2, O2, K2
Row 18: O, K2tog, K5, P1, K9, P1, K10, O, K2tog, K4, P1, K5, O, K2tog,
         K2
Row 19: Sp, K3, O, K2tog, A2, K2, O, K2tog, K2, K2tog, O, K1, A2,
         K2, A2, K1, O2, K2
Row 20: O, K2tog, K4, P1, K3, P1, K5, P1, K3, P1, K8, O, K2tog, K2,
         (P1, K3)2, O, K2tog, K2
Row 21: Sp, K3, O, K2tog, K2, A, K4, O, K2tog, K1, K2tog, O, K4, A,
         K6, A, K4, O2, K2
Row 22: O, K2tog, K7, P1, K9, P1, K10, O, K2tog, K4, P1, K5, O,
         K2tog, K2
Row 23: Sp, K3, O, K2tog, A2, K2, O, K2tog, K3, O, K2tog, A2, K2, A3, K1
Row 24: O, K2tog, K4, P1, K3, P1, K5, P1, K3, P1, K8, O, K2tog, K2,
         P1, K3, P1, K3, O, K2tog, K2
Row 25: Sp, K3, O, K2tog, K2, A, K4, O, K2tog, K4, O, K2tog, K1, A,
         K6, (A, K1)2
Row 26: O, K2tog, K5, P1, K9, P1, K10, O, K2tog, K4, P1, K5, O,
         K2tog, K2
Row 27: Sp, K3, O, K2tog, K10, O, K2tog, K5, O, K2tog, K5, A, K5, A, K1
Row 28: O, K2tog, K9, P1, K15, O, K2tog, K10, O, K2tog, K2
Row 29: Sp, K3, O, K2tog, K10, O, K2tog, K6, O, K2tog, K2, A2, K2, A, K1
Row 30: O, K2tog, K6, P1, K3, P1, K13, O, K2tog, K10, O, K2tog, K2
Row 31: Sp, K3, O, K2tog, K2, A, K4, O, K2tog, K7, O, K2tog, K3, A,
         K3, A, K1
Row 32: O, K2tog, K7, P1, K15, O, K2tog, K4, P1, K5, O, K2tog, K2
Row 33: Sp, K3, O, K2tog, A2, K2, O, K2tog, K8, O, K2tog, A3, K1
Row 34: O, K2tog, K4, P1, K3, P1, K13, O, K2tog, K2, (P1,K3)2, O,
         K2tog, K2
Row 35: Sp, K3, O, K2tog, K2, A, K4, O, K2tog, K9, O, K2tog, K1,(A,K1)2
Row 36: O, K2tog, K5, P1, K15, O, K2tog, K4, P1, K5, O, K2tog, K2
Row 37: Sp, K3, O, K2tog, A2, K2, O, K2tog, K10, O, K2tog, K4, A, K1
Row 38: O, K2tog, K20, O, K2tog, K2, (P1, K3)2, O, K2tog, K2
Row 39: Sp, K3, O, K2tog, K2, A, K4, O, K2tog, K11, O, K2tog, K2, A, K1
Row 40: O, K2tog, K19, O, K2tog, K4, P1, K5, O, K2tog, K2
Row 41: Sp, K3, O, K2tog, K10, O, K2tog, K12, O, K2tog, A, K1
Row 42: O, K2tog, K18, O, K2tog, K10, O, K2tog, K2

WIDE OPEN BORDER

Work on a pair of needles
Cast on 16 stitches and knit 1 row

Row 1:   Sp, K3, (02, K2tog)6
Row 2:   (K2, P1)6, K4
Row 3:   Sp, K3, (02, K2tog)9
Row 4:   (K2, P1)9, K4
Row 5:   Sp, K3, 02, K2tog, (0, K2tog)12, K1
Row 6:   K27, P1, K4
Row 7:   Sp, K3, 02, K2tog, (0, K2tog)13
Row 8:   K28, P1, K4
Row 9:   Sp, K3, 02, K2tog, (0, K2tog)13, 0, K1
Row 10:   K30, P1, K4
Row 11:   K35
Row 12:   C10, (K2tog)9, K6

PATTERN REPEAT:
Repeat rows 1 to 12

Twilley's Lyscordet No 5, 2.5 mm (12) needles:
41 cm (16") x 10 cm (4") took 25 gm (1 Oz) yarn

Each pattern repeat took an average of 12 minutes to knit.